17th Conference of the European Chapter of the Association for Computational Linguistics (EACL 2023)

Tutorial Abstracts

Dubrovnik, Croatia
2-4 May 2023

ISBN: 978-1-7138-7378-5

Printed from e-media with permission by:

Curran Associates, Inc.
57 Morehouse Lane
Red Hook, NY 12571

Some format issues inherent in the e-media version may also appear in this print version.

Association for Computational Linguistics
209 N. Eighth Street
Stroudsburg, Pennsylvania 18360

Phone: 1-570-476-8006
Fax: 1-570-476-0860

acl@aclweb.org

Additional copies of this publication are available from:

Curran Associates, Inc.
57 Morehouse Lane
Red Hook, NY 12571 USA
Phone: 845-758-0400
Fax: 845-758-2633
Email: curran@proceedings.com
Web: www.proceedings.com

EACL 2023

The 17th Conference of the European Chapter of the Association for Computational Linguistics

Proceedings of Tutorial Abstracts

May 2-4, 2023

The EACL organizers gratefully acknowledge the support from the following sponsors.

Diamond and Welcome Event

grammarly

Diamond

LIVEPERSON

Platinum and D&I Ally

amazon | science

Platinum

Bloomberg
Engineering

Silver

Bronze

Introduction

Welcome to the Tutorials Session of EACL 2022.

NLP is a rapidly-changing field, which has undergone different periods, and the knowledge needed to be at pace is changing rapidly. The EACL tutorial session is organized to give conference attendees an introduction by expert researchers to some topics of importance drawn from our rapidly growing and changing research field.

This year, as has been the tradition over the past few years, the call, submission, reviewing, and selection of tutorials were coordinated jointly for multiple conferences: ACL, EACL, and EMNLP.
We would like to thank the tutorial authors for their contributions and flexibility while organizing the conference in the hybrid mode.

We hope you enjoy the tutorials while Understanding Ethics, Preserving Privacy, and Analyzing Emotions in NLP and while Summarizing Dialogues, Mining Arguments, and Learning AutoML.

EACL 2022 Tutorial Co-chairs
Fabio Massimo Zanzotto
Sameer Pradhan

Organizing Committee

General Chair

Alessandro Moschitti, Amazon Alexa

Program Chairs

Isabelle Augenstein, University of Copenhagen
Andreas Vlachos, University of Cambridge

Tutorial Chairs

Fabio Massimo Zanzotto, University of Rome Tor Vergata
Sameer Pradhan, cemantix.org

Table of Contents

Mining, Assessing, and Improving Arguments in NLP and the Social Sciences

Gabriella Lapesa[1], **Eva Maria Vecchi**[1], **Serena Villata**[2], **Henning Wachsmuth**[3]
[1]University of Stuttgart, Institute for Natural Language Processing
[2]Université Côte d'Azur, Inria, CNRS, I3S,
[3]Leibniz University Hannover, Institute of Artificial Intelligence
name.surname@ims.uni-stuttgart.de
villata@i3S.unice.fr, h.wachsmuth@ai.uni-hannover.de

Abstract

Computational argumentation is an interdisciplinary research field, connecting Natural Language Processing (NLP) to other disciplines such as the social sciences. This tutorial will focus on a task that recently got into the center of attention in the community: *argument quality assessment*, that is, what makes an argument good or bad? We structure the tutorial along three main coordinates: (1) the notions of argument quality across disciplines (how do we recognize good and bad arguments?), (2) the modeling of subjectivity (who argues to whom; what are their beliefs?), and (3) the generation of improved arguments (what makes an argument better?). The tutorial highlights interdisciplinary aspects of the field, ranging from the collaboration of theory and practice (e.g., in NLP and social sciences), to approaching different types of linguistic structures (e.g., social media versus parliamentary texts), and facing the ethical issues involved (e.g., how to build applications for the social good). A key feature of this tutorial is its interactive nature: We will involve the participants in two annotation studies on the assessment and the improvement of quality, and we will encourage them to reflect on the challenges and potential of these tasks.

1 Introduction

Computational argumentation is a field encompassing varying tasks on the automated analysis and synthesis of natural language arguments. Until recently, research in Natural Language Processing (NLP) mostly dealt with *Argument Mining* (AM), that is, the identification of argumentative claims that convey a stance towards some controversial issue, along with evidence given as reasons for the claims. AM has been studied for various genres (Mochales and Moens, 2011; Habernal and Gurevych, 2017; Dusmanu et al., 2017a) and argument models (Toulmin, 1958; Walton et al., 2008; Freeman, 2011). As Lawrence and Reed (2019) point out, the "reason giving" function of argumentation is what makes AM specific: "Although opinion mining and sentiment analysis provide techniques that are proving to be enormously successful [...] they can only tell us what opinions are being expressed and not why people hold the opinions they do". *Reason giving*, however, is only one of two main functions of argumentation, the other being *persuasion*. The dynamics of these "two souls" of argumentation are complex and the balance between reason giving and persuasion varies depending on the communication setting.

Mining Arguments In this tutorial, we start from the body of research on AM. Unlike recent NLP tutorials on argumentation (Budzynska and Reed, 2019; Bar-Haim et al., 2021), however, our focus is a task that recently got into the center of attention: *argument quality assessment*, that is, to rate or to compare how good arguments are with respect to one or more defined quality dimensions.

The NLP Perspective: Assessing Argument Quality Let us start with the concrete example of argument quality annotations in Figure 1, taken from Lauscher et al. (2020). The topic is "freedom of speech", and the stance is "against" (i.e., the government has the right to censorship). Quality is assessed here in four dimensions: *cogency* (is the conclusion adequately supported with relevant and sufficient premises?), *effectiveness* (how persuasive is the argument?), *reasonableness* (is the argument good in the context of the debate in which it is framed?), and *overall quality*.

The example illustrates the challenges which we take as coordinates of this tutorial. The first challenge is the identification and definition of appropriate *dimensions* for quality assessment: for example, in this case, the effectiveness label conflates several aspects. The second challenge in quality assessment is *subjectivity*. In our example, the three annotators (linguistics experts) clearly disagree in their assessment. Lauscher et al. (2020)

Proceedings of the 17th Conference of the European Chapter of the Association for Computational Linguistics
Tutorial Abstracts, pages 1–6

Title: *Should 'blogging' be a capital crime? Iran is considering it...*
Stance: *A government has the right to censor speech (...)*

Text: *My government doesn't give me freedom of speech, so I have to argue for this side. Freedom of speech is bad because ... um ... then Our Leader's beliefs could be challenged. No one wants that. I mean, if everyone would just say and believe what Our Leader says to, we wouldn't need those firing squads altogether! Everyone wins.*

	Cogency	Effectiveness	Reasonableness	Overall
Annotator 1	4	1	1	2
Annotator 2	4	5	3	4
Annotator 3	2	2	2	2

Figure 1: Argument quality assessment from Lauscher et al. (2020): Example argument, annotated for four dimensions by three annotators, with partial agreement.

report that a crucial factor of disagreement of Annotators 1 and 2 was their perception of the ironic tone behind the text. Interestingly, for both of them, the text has a medium-high degree of cogency (so it is logically pretty "healthy"). A further challenge would be to improve the quality of this argument: How would we make this argument more effective? Do we need more irony, less irony, or a stronger statement of the stance?

To inform participants about argument quality, the tutorial will systematically review existing research on argument quality based on the literature (Wachsmuth et al., 2017), outlining the subjectiveness of quality dimensions as a key problem. In an interactive annotation session, participants will explore and discuss the assessment of quality on real-life arguments. They will be encouraged to take a critical standpoint to the annotation guidelines, learning in a concrete scenario how difficult it is to establish a trade-off between expressivity of the annotation schema and feasibility of the task.

The Social Science Perspective: Assessing Deliberative Quality To demonstrate the impact of argument quality in practice, the tutorial will bridge research in NLP with the social sciences, looking at deliberative democracy in particular. Deliberative democracy is an approach to democratic processes which does not focus on the output of decision-making, but on the discourse exchange that precedes it (Bächtiger and Parkinson, 2019). Crucially, deliberative theory scholars have been asking the same question as computational argumentation: What makes a contribution to a discussion good? This has led to the development of a *discourse quality index* to assess the quality of a discourse contribution (Steenbergen et al., 2003; Gerber et al., 2016). While the dimensions of the index partially overlap with argument quality dimensions, some bring in a different perspective, for example, whether the discourse participants make reference to "common good" or whether they engage with other participants.

Modeling Subjectivity Next, we will deal with subjectivity, modeling the parties involved in debates along with their values and beliefs. The connections of argument quality and deliberative quality highlight the subjective nature of argumentation, one of the three main coordinates of this tutorial. Subjectivity has been the trigger of an "affective turn" in both deliberative theory and computational argumentation. In the former, this has implied a switch from a purely rational perspective on deliberation to one which incorporates emotions, personal narratives, humor (Hoggett and Thompson, 2002; Black, 2020; Esau, 2018; Esau and Friess, 2022). In the latter, the affective turn has brought personal argumentation at center stage, highlighting the role played by human values (Kiesel et al., 2022), moral discourse (Alshomary et al., 2022), and narratives (Falk and Lapesa, 2022).

In the tutorial, we aim to foster participants to reflect on the two-fold role that subjectivity plays in quality assessment: subjective factors in quality assessment (e.g., interpretation of humor, as in the example above), and subjective factors in the production of an argument (e.g., all the "personal argumentation" ingredients listed before).

Improving Arguments The subjectivity topic will lead to another interactive session where the goal is to improve the quality of arguments. Limitations will be discussed as well as first research on quality-related argument generation (Gurcke et al., 2021; Skitalinskaya et al., 2022), before the tutorial concludes with an outlook on future perspectives.

2 Diversity

We believe that exposing the students to the deliberative perspective of argumentation will be fruitful and enriching, as it might not be known to the typical *CL audience. It is our goal that participants leave our tutorial having learned the value of taking multiple disciplinary perspectives into account, even in a rather technical (logic- and NLP-oriented) subject such as computational argumentation. Besides, our focus on subjectivity and personal argumentation as positive features (and not bugs) brings individuals and their differences at center stage, contributing to inclusivity in the field.

3 Learning Outcomes

This introductory tutorial aims to offer an elaborate, systematic, and interdisciplinary understanding of the assessment and improvement of the quality of natural language arguments:

- Basics of argument mining, computational models of argumentation, argument quality assessment, and argument generation;
- Understanding of the NLP perspective: impact of assessing argument quality in practice;
- Understanding of the social sciences perspective: goals of deliberation (cooperative decision making) and real-world applications;
- Hands-on experience on the challenges of assessing and improving argument quality.

4 Tutorial Outline

Part I (60 min.) Mining Arguments

- Overview of computational argumentation
- Argument mining: Humans vs. computers
- Achieved results and open challenges

Part II (60 min.) The NLP Perspective: Assessing Argument Quality

- What makes an argument "good"?
- Logical, rhetorical, and dialectical dimensions of argument quality
- Subjectiveness as the key challenge for annotation and modeling
- Discussion of the notions of argument quality: Are they sufficient? Are they all necessary?

Part III (60 min.) Interactive Session 1

- Annotation: Assessment of sample arguments
- Consolidation: To what extent participants agree? Where not, and why?
- Discussion: What are alternative strategies to subjective quality annotation?

Part IV (45 min.) The Social Sciences Perspective: Assessing Deliberative Quality

- Direct democracy, deliberative theories, and e-deliberation
- Deliberative quality: Features and annotation
- Integration of deliberative features in computational architectures
- Application: Argument quality for social good

Part V (30 min.) Modeling Subjectivity

- Authors, audiences, and third parties
- Human values, moral foundations, narratives
- Issues with subjectivity

Part VI (60 min.) Interactive Session 2

- Annotation: Rewriting of sample arguments
- Consolidation: What was improved and how?
- Discussion: What can be improved, what not?

Part VII (45 min.) Improving Argument Quality

- Generation methods for improving arguments
- Challenges and lessons learned
- Conclusions and next steps for the field

5 Tutorial Breadth

The key objective of this tutorial is to provide a comprehensive overview of recent and current research on the assessment and improvement of quality in computational argumentation, in both NLP and the social sciences. We estimate that at most one quarter of the tutorial will cover our own work.

6 Presenters

Gabriella Lapesa leads the research group E-DELIB (*Powering-up E-DELIBeration: towards AI-supported moderation*) at the Institute for Natural Language Processing, University of Stuttgart. Her group works at the intersection between NLP (AM) and social science (Deliberative Theory) to develop methods and tools to support moderators in deliberative discussion. As a research associate in the project MARDY (*Modeling ARgumentation Dynamics in Political Discourse*, University of Stuttgart and Bremen), she works on NLP methods to scale-up the analysis policy debates in multiple textual sources (i.e., who claims what in the debate on immigration or Covid-19?). Gabriella has co-chaired the 9th Argument Mining workshop (2022). With Eva Maria Vecchi, she co-taught a course on interdisciplinary AM at ESSLLI 2022.[1]

Eva Maria Vecchi has a background in linguistics and mathematics and holds a Ph.D. degree in cognitive and neurosciences. She is a postdoctoral researcher at the Institute for Natural Language Processing at IMS Stuttgart, working on the E-DELIB

[1]https://sites.google.com/view/esslli2022-am-in-nlp-ss/

project. Her focus is on the interdisciplinary effort between NLP techniques for argument mining (AM) and theories in the social sciences with the goal of a more collaborative, productive, and ethical endeavor for e-Deliberation. She has taught courses and tutorials on AM and other topics, most recently with Gabriella Lapesa at ESSLLI 2022. Her current research aims at a better understanding of the role bias has in computational argumentation and e-Deliberation, particularly the impact it has on the models, implementation, and social aspects of computational argumentation.

Serena Villata is a research director in computer science at CNRS, and she pursues her research at the I3S laboratory in Sophia Antipolis (France). Her research area is computational argumentation, with a focus on legal and medical texts, political debates and social network harmful content (abusive language, disinformation). Her work conjugates argument-based reasoning frameworks with natural language arguments extracted from text. She is the author of over 150 scientific publications on the topic. She holds a Chair of the Interdisciplinary Institute for AI 3IA Côte d'Azur on "Artificial Argumentation for Humans". Serena has co-chaired the 7th Workshop on Argument Mining at COLING 2020. She has also given tutorials on Argument Mining at ESSLLI 2017[2] and IJCAI 2016[3].

Henning Wachsmuth is the head of the Natural Language Processing Group at Leibniz University Hannover. He is an internationally leading researcher on computational argumentation with more than 60 publications on the topic, many at major NLP and AI venues. Other interests include social bias mitigation, computational reframing, and explainable NLP. Henning has co-chaired the 6th Workshop on Argument Mining at ACL 2019, and has given tutorials on argumentation at ASIRF 2018 (Cole and Achilles, 2019), EuroCSS 2018,[4] KI 2019 (Benzmüller and Stuckenschmidt, 2019), and KI 2020 (Schmid et al., 2020). He is an initiator of the CLEF shared task series Touché on argument retrieval (Bondarenko et al., 2022), and co-chaired SemEval tasks on argument reasoning comprehension (Habernal et al., 2018), propaganda technique detection (Da San Martino et al., 2020), and identifying human values in arguments.[5]

7 Target Audience / Prerequisites

The tutorial targets both participants who are new to the field of computational argumentation and those who need a comprehensive overview of techniques and applications. As the tutorial is interdisciplinary by design, it is also of interest to participants from a social sciences background who hope to integrate their knowledge within NLP. Finally, we expect the tutorial to attract attention from people interested in NLP techniques that currently impact the social and political world, in general. Basic knowledge of linguistics and computational linguistics is required. A general interest in the collaboration between NLP and social sciences is expected; relevant material, however, will be introduced without requiring prior knowledge.

8 Other Information

Tutorial Type: Introductory, 6 hours
Tutorial Materials: Tutorial materials and related information will be made available online.

9 Recommended Reading List

Survey Papers (Cabrio and Villata, 2018; Lawrence and Reed, 2019; Vecchi et al., 2021)
Mining Arguments (Habernal and Gurevych, 2017; Daxenberger et al., 2017; Dusmanu et al., 2017b)
Assessing Argument Quality (Wachsmuth et al., 2017; Lauscher et al., 2020; Marro et al., 2022)
Assessing Deliberative Quality (Steenbergen et al., 2003; Gerber et al., 2016)
Improving Arguments (Hua and Wang, 2018; Alshomary et al., 2020; Gurcke et al., 2021)
Challenges (Durmus et al., 2019; Toledo-Ronen et al., 2020; Spliethöver and Wachsmuth, 2020)

Acknowledgments

Gabriella Lapesa and Eva Maria Vecchi are funded by the Bundesministerium für Bildung und Forschung (BMBF), project E-DELIB (*Powering up E-deliberation: towards AI-supported moderation*). Serena Villata is supported by the French government, through the 3IA Côte d'Azur Investments in the Future project managed by the ANR with the reference number ANR-19-P3IA-0002.

[2] https://www.irit.fr/esslli2017/courses/39.html
[3] https://ijcai-16.org/index.php/welcome/view/accepted_tutorials/
[4] http://symposium.computationalsocialscience.eu/2018/
[5] Ongoing task found here: https://touche.webis.de/semeval23/touche23-web

References

Milad Alshomary, Roxanne El Baff, Timon Gurcke, and Henning Wachsmuth. 2022. The moral debater: A study on the computational generation of morally framed arguments. In *Proceedings of the 60th Annual Meeting of the Association for Computational Linguistics (Volume 1: Long Papers)*, pages 8782–8797, Dublin, Ireland. Association for Computational Linguistics.

Milad Alshomary, Shahbaz Syed, Martin Potthast, and Henning Wachsmuth. 2020. Target inference in argument conclusion generation. In *Proceedings of the 58th Annual Meeting of the Association for Computational Linguistics*, pages 4334–4345, Online. Association for Computational Linguistics.

Andre Bächtiger and John Parkinson. 2019. *Towards a New Deliberative Quality*. Oxford University Press, Cambridge, MA, USA.

Roy Bar-Haim, Liat Ein-Dor, Matan Orbach, Elad Venezian, and Noam Slonim. 2021. Advances in debating technologies: Building AI that can debate humans. In *Proceedings of the 59th Annual Meeting of the Association for Computational Linguistics and the 11th International Joint Conference on Natural Language Processing: Tutorial Abstracts*, pages 1–5, Online. Association for Computational Linguistics.

Christoph Benzmüller and Heiner Stuckenschmidt, editors. 2019. *KI 2019: Advances in Artificial Intelligence - 42nd German Conference on AI, Kassel, Germany, September 23-26, 2019, Proceedings*, volume 11793 of *Lecture Notes in Computer Science*. Springer.

Laura Black. 2020. Framing democracy and conflict through storytelling in deliberative groups. *Regular Issue*, 9(1).

Alexander Bondarenko, Maik Fröbe, Johannes Kiesel, Shahbaz Syed, Timon Gurcke, Meriem Beloucif, Alexander Panchenko, Chris Biemann, Benno Stein, Henning Wachsmuth, Martin Potthast, and Matthias Hagen. 2022. Overview of touché 2022: ArgumentÂ retrieval. In *Experimental IR Meets Multilinguality, Multimodality, and Interaction*, pages 311–336, Cham. Springer International Publishing.

Katarzyna Budzynska and Chris Reed. 2019. Advances in argument mining. In *Proceedings of the 57th Annual Meeting of the Association for Computational Linguistics: Tutorial Abstracts*, pages 39–42, Florence, Italy. Association for Computational Linguistics.

Elena Cabrio and S. Villata. 2018. Five years of argument mining: a data-driven analysis. In *Proceedings of the Twenty-Seventh International Joint Conference on Artificial Intelligence, IJCAI 2018*, pages 5427–5433.

Amelia W. Cole and Linda Achilles. 2019. Autumn school for information retrieval and foraging 2018. *SIGIR Forum*, 52(2):87?91.

Giovanni Da San Martino, Alberto Barrón-Cedeño, Henning Wachsmuth, Rostislav Petrov, and Preslav Nakov. 2020. SemEval-2020 task 11: Detection of propaganda techniques in news articles. In *14th International Workshop on Semantic Evaluation (SemEval 2020)*, pages 1377–1414, Barcelona (online). Association for Computational Linguistics.

Johannes Daxenberger, Steffen Eger, Ivan Habernal, Christian Stab, and Iryna Gurevych. 2017. What is the essence of a claim? cross-domain claim identification. In *Proceedings of the 2017 Conference on Empirical Methods in Natural Language Processing*, pages 2055–2066, Copenhagen, Denmark. Association for Computational Linguistics.

Esin Durmus, Faisal Ladhak, and Claire Cardie. 2019. The role of pragmatic and discourse context in determining argument impact. In *Proceedings of the 2019 Conference on Empirical Methods in Natural Language Processing and the 9th International Joint Conference on Natural Language Processing (EMNLP-IJCNLP)*, pages 5668–5678, Hong Kong, China. Association for Computational Linguistics.

Mihai Dusmanu, Elena Cabrio, and Serena Villata. 2017a. Argument mining on Twitter: Arguments, facts and sources. In *Proceedings of the 2017 Conference on Empirical Methods in Natural Language Processing*, pages 2317–2322, Copenhagen, Denmark. Association for Computational Linguistics.

Mihai Dusmanu, Elena Cabrio, and Serena Villata. 2017b. Argument mining on twitter: Arguments, facts and sources. In *Proceedings of the 2017 Conference on Empirical Methods in Natural Language Processing*, pages 2317–2322.

Katharina Esau. 2018. Capturing citizens' values: On the role of narratives and emotions in digital participation. *Analyse & Kritik*, 40(1):55–72.

Katharina Esau and Daniel Friess. 2022. What creates listening online? exploring reciprocity in online political discussions with relational content analysis. *Journal of Deliberative Democracy*, 18(1):1–16.

Neele Falk and Gabriella Lapesa. 2022. Reports of personal experiences and stories in argumentation: datasets and analysis. In *Proceedings of the 60th Annual Meeting of the Association for Computational Linguistics (Volume 1: Long Papers)*, pages 5530–5553, Dublin, Ireland. Association for Computational Linguistics.

James B. Freeman. 2011. *Argument Structure: Representation and Theory*. Springer.

Marlené Gerber, André Bächtiger, Susumu Shikano, Simon Reber, and Samuel Rohr. 2016. Deliberative abilities and influence in a transnational deliberative poll (europolis). *British Journal of Political Science*, 48(4):1093–1118.

Timon Gurcke, Milad Alshomary, and Henning Wachsmuth. 2021. Assessing the sufficiency of arguments through conclusion generation. In *Proceedings of the 8th Workshop on Argument Mining*, pages 67–77, Punta Cana, Dominican Republic. Association for Computational Linguistics.

Ivan Habernal and Iryna Gurevych. 2017. Argumentation mining in user-generated web discourse. *Computational Linguistics*, 43(1).

Ivan Habernal, Henning Wachsmuth, Iryna Gurevych, and Benno Stein. 2018. SemEval 2018 Task 12: The Argument Reasoning Comprehension Task. In *12th International Workshop on Semantic Evaluation (SemEval 2018)*. Association for Computational Linguistics.

Paul Hoggett and Simon Thompson. 2002. Toward a democracy of the emotions. *Constellations*, 9(1):106–126.

Xinyu Hua and Lu Wang. 2018. Neural argument generation augmented with externally retrieved evidence. In *Proceedings of the 56th Annual Meeting of the Association for Computational Linguistics (Volume 1: Long Papers)*, pages 219–230, Melbourne, Australia. Association for Computational Linguistics.

Johannes Kiesel, Milad Alshomary, Nicolas Handke, Xiaoni Cai, Henning Wachsmuth, and Benno Stein. 2022. Identifying the human values behind arguments. In *Proceedings of the 60th Annual Meeting of the Association for Computational Linguistics (Volume 1: Long Papers)*, pages 4459–4471, Dublin, Ireland. Association for Computational Linguistics.

Anne Lauscher, Lily Ng, Courtney Napoles, and Joel Tetreault. 2020. Rhetoric, logic, and dialectic: Advancing theory-based argument quality assessment in natural language processing. In *Proceedings of the 28th International Conference on Computational Linguistics*, pages 4563–4574, Barcelona, Spain (Online). International Committee on Computational Linguistics.

John Lawrence and Chris Reed. 2019. Argument mining: A survey. *Computational Linguistics*, 45(4):765–818.

Santiago Marro, Elena Cabrio, and Serena Villata. 2022. Graph embeddings for argumentation quality assessment. In *Findings of EMNLP*.

Raquel Mochales and Marie-Francine Moens. 2011. Argumentation mining. *Artificial Intelligence and Law*, 19(1):1–22.

Ute Schmid, Franziska Klügl, , and Diedrich Wolter, editors. 2020. *KI 2020: Advances in Artificial Intelligence: 43rd German Conference on AI, Bamberg, Germany, September 21–25, 2020, Proceedings*. Springer-Verlag, Berlin, Heidelberg.

Gabriella Skitalinskaya, Maximilian Spliethöver, and Henning Wachsmuth. 2022. Claim optimization in computational argumentation.

Maximilian Spliethöver and Henning Wachsmuth. 2020. Argument from old man's view: Assessing social bias in argumentation. In *Proceedings of the 7th Workshop on Argument Mining*, pages 76–87, Online. Association for Computational Linguistics.

M. Steenbergen, Andre Baechtiger, Markus Spörndli, and J. Steiner. 2003. Measuring political deliberation: A discourse quality index. *Comparative European Politics*, 1:21–48.

Orith Toledo-Ronen, Matan Orbach, Yonatan Bilu, Artem Spector, and Noam Slonim. 2020. Multilingual argument mining: Datasets and analysis. In *Findings of the Association for Computational Linguistics: EMNLP 2020*, pages 303–317, Online. Association for Computational Linguistics.

Stephen E. Toulmin. 1958. *The Uses of Argument*. Cambridge University Press.

Eva Maria Vecchi, Neele Falk, Iman Jundi, and Gabriella Lapesa. 2021. Towards argument mining for social good: A survey. In *Proceedings of the 59th Annual Meeting of the Association for Computational Linguistics and the 11th International Joint Conference on Natural Language Processing (Volume 1: Long Papers)*, pages 1338–1352.

Henning Wachsmuth, Nona Naderi, Yufang Hou, Yonatan Bilu, Vinodkumar Prabhakaran, Tim Alberdingk Thijm, Graeme Hirst, and Benno Stein. 2017. Computational argumentation quality assessment in natural language. In *Proceedings of the 15th Conference of the European Chapter of the Association for Computational Linguistics: Volume 1, Long Papers*, pages 176–187, Valencia, Spain. Association for Computational Linguistics.

Douglas Walton, Christopher Reed, and Fabrizio Macagno. 2008. *Argumentation Schemes*. Cambridge University Press.

Emotion Analysis in Texts

Sanja Štajner
Karlsruhe, Germany
stajner.sanja@gmail.com

Roman Klinger
Institut für Maschinelle Sprachverarbeitung
University of Stuttgart, Germany
roman.klinger@ims.uni-stuttgart.de

Abstract

Emotion analysis in text is an area of research that encompasses a set of various natural language processing (NLP) tasks, including classification and regression settings, as well as structured prediction tasks like role labeling or stimulus detection. In this tutorial, we provide an overview of research from emotion psychology which sets the ground for choosing adequate NLP methodology, and present existing resources and classification methods used for emotion analysis in texts. We further discuss appraisal theories and how events can be interpreted regarding their presumably caused emotion and briefly introduce emotion role labeling. In addition to these technical topics, we discuss the use cases of emotion analysis in text, their societal impact, ethical considerations, as well as the main challenges in the field.

1 Description and Relevance

Automatic emotion detection in texts has been gaining popularity since 2010's (Acheampong et al., 2020). The systems for automatic emotion detection are often used on social media posts for public opinion analysis, e.g. with respect to climate change (Loureiro and Alló, 2020), to obtain better consumer insights (Sykora et al., 2022), enhance prediction of corporate financial performance (Wang et al., 2023), or predict outcome of elections (Srinivasan et al., 2019). Automatic emotion detection systems are also envisioned to have an important role in building empathetic chatbots and virtual agents (Paiva et al., 2017; Rashkin et al., 2019; Lin et al., 2019b; Shin et al., 2019; Lin et al., 2019a; Ma et al., 2020). More importantly, emotion analysis could be used to aid suicide prevention (Pestian et al., 2012; Desmet and Hoste, 2013), and depression detection (Deshpande and Rao, 2017; Shanthi et al., 2022).

In the computational linguistics (CL) research community, the most commonly used emotion models are Ekman's model (Ekman and Friesen, 1981) consisting of six basic emotions (*anger*, *disgust*, *fear*, *joy*, *sadness*, and *surprise*), and Plutchik's model (Plutchik, 1982), which is commonly used focusing on eight primary emotions (*anger*, *anticipation*, *disgust*, *fear*, *joy*, *sadness*, *surprise*, and *trust*). However, some studies opt for different emotion frameworks or customized emotion sets. For example, Brynielsson et al. (2014), Mohammad et al. (2015), Demszky et al. (2020), Bostan et al. (2020), and Huguet Cabot et al. (2021) use customized emotion sets, Neviarouskaya et al. (2010) use attitudes, and Troiano et al. (2023) use appraisals. Since 2005, over 15 datasets manually annotated for emotions has been compiled and made freely available. The majority of datasets is in English, and they cover a variety of domains and text types: Twitter data (Schuff et al., 2017; Mohammad et al., 2015); personal reports on emotional events (Scherer and Wallbott, 1994; Troiano et al., 2019); sentences from fairy tales (Alm et al., 2005); daily dialogs from websites for English language learners (Li et al., 2017); dialog utterances from the television sitcom Friends (Hsu et al., 2018); movie subtitles (Öhman et al., 2020); news headlines (Bostan et al., 2020; Strapparava and Mihalcea, 2007); and Reddit comments (Demszky et al., 2020; Huguet Cabot et al., 2021). The XED dataset (Öhman et al., 2020), a manually annotated dataset of movies subtitles in English and Finish has been extended to 35 further languages by annotation projection to the parallel sentences in those languages.

From the computational perspective, the research community has used a wide range of approaches for emotion detection and classification, e.g., traditional machine learning approaches that use emotion dictionaries (Mohammad et al., 2015), linear classifiers with various lexical, syntactic, semantic, and structural features (Alm et al., 2005), maximum entropy classifiers with bag-of-words as features (Bostan and Klinger, 2018), support vector machines and naïve Bayes classifiers with

Proceedings of the 17th Conference of the European Chapter of the Association for Computational Linguistics
Tutorial Abstracts, pages 7–12

various lexical, syntactic, and semantic features (Brynielsson et al., 2014), CNN-based classifiers (Hsu et al., 2018), BERT-based classifiers (Demszky et al., 2020; Öhman et al., 2020), multi-task learning (Huguet Cabot et al., 2021), zero-shot learning (Plaza-del Arco et al., 2022; Gebremichael Tesfagergish et al., 2022), and few-shot learning (Guibon et al., 2021). Given that different architectures were tested on different domains, text types, and class types and distributions, it is not clear which models should be considered state of the art. Commercial emotion analysis models commonly use either dictionary-based approaches (due to their domain customisation capabilities which do not require large amounts of labelled training data) or BERT-based models (due to their domain-agnostic adaptation capabilities in the case of sufficient amounts of labelled training data).

Since 2010's, CL research community has been exponentially increasing the effort in building models for recognising and discerning among Ekman's or Plutchik's basic emotions in texts (Acheampong et al., 2020), and building manually annotated datasets, despite of studies in emotion psychology which suggested that detecting emotions in text is difficult and unreliable (Plutchik, 2001; Lang, 2010). The CL studies have pointed out several challenges in emotion annotation in texts: missing context in short utterances (Öhman et al., 2020; Mohammad, 2012), non-literal meaning (Mohammad, 2012), different perspectives one may take, i.e., the reader's, writer's, or text's (Buechel and Hahn, 2017; Alm et al., 2005), and high subjectivity of the task (low inter-annotator agreements were found even among trained annotators (Alm et al., 2005; Schuff et al., 2017; Štajner, 2021)).

Despite the various challenges in emotion analysis from texts, which were reported by researches in emotion psychology or natural language processing (NLP), many tools for emotion analysis are available without a thorough description of challenges and failure modes, e.g. Text2emotion[1] and NRCLex[2] Python libraries. A large number of for-profit companies offer emotion analysis from texts, either using pre-trained models, or customised models trained on clients' data, e.g. BytesView[3], Komprehend[4], IBM Watson Natural Language Understanding.[5] When using the paid emotion analysis APIs, the identification of failure modes on specific datasets or in specific applications, the risk of unintended harms and other ethical considerations are usually shifted to the user of APIs. Those tasks then become extremely difficult given that companies that offer paid APIs often do not disclose the model specifications and datasets the models were trained on.

This tutorial has several goals. First, it provides an overview of most commonly used emotion models and their grounding in emotion psychology, their limitation and challenges from a psychological perspective as well as from NLP perspective. Second, it provides an extensive overview of freely available emotion analysis datasets, their annotation strategies and limitations. Third, it provides an extensive overview and critical comparison of NLP models used for emotion analysis in texts, ranging from traditional machine learning classifiers based on emotion dictionaries to transformer-based classification systems and zero-shot and few-shot learning models. Finally, this tutorial aims at raising awareness about various ethical issues concerning emotion analysis and the still present challenges in emotion analysis in texts (the absence of standardized annotation and evaluation procedures, common failure modes, etc.) which need to be considered when using emotion analysis in real-world applications to avoid unintended harms.

To provide the tutorial participants with a better understanding of the challenges in emotion analysis and help them get started with developing novel models for emotion analysis, we will implement (at the end of the second part of the tutorial) a small annotation exercise.

2 Type: cutting-edge

The first part of the tutorial is an introduction to emotion psychology and the use cases of emotion analysis. The second and third part of the tutorial present cutting-edge NLP research on emotion analysis in texts.

[1] https://pypi.org/project/text2emotion/

[2] https://pypi.org/project/NRCLex/

[3] https://www.bytesview.com/emotion-analysis

[4] https://komprehend.io/emotion-analysis

[5] https://www.ibm.com/cloud/watson-natural-language-understanding

3 Target Audience

This tutorial is well-suited for various audiences: junior and senior researches working on emotion annotation and evaluation of emotion detection models; junior and senior researches working on novel models for emotion analysis, especially those using deep-learning paradigms; industry practitioners who wish to better understand limitations of publicly available emotion analysis tools and models. There are no prerequisites for attending. However, to fully understand the discussion about strengths and limitations of different computational models, a basic knowledge of commonly used non-neural and neural classifiers is recommended.

4 Tutorial Structure

This tutorial contains three thematic parts, each to be covered in a one-hour time slot. The first part introduces emotion models, findings of relevant psychological studies, and use cases. The second part focuses on existing datasets for emotion analysis in texts, and strengths and weaknesses of the computational models which have been proposed so far. The third part covers the fine-grained emotion analysis tasks such as emotion role labeling and stimulus detection, as well as the interpretation of events with appraisal theories. In this part, we also discuss the main challenges in emotion analysis in texts, and ethical considerations for its real-world applications.

Part 1: Foundations

- Emotion theories in psychology
- Emotion recognition reliability in vision and language and what we can expect in NLP
- Use cases and social impact

Part 2: Resources and Computational Models

- Resources for emotion classification
- Resources for emotion intensity prediction
- Non-neural models
- Multi-task and transfer-based models
- Zero-shot and few-shot learning
- Interactive annotation exercise

Part 3: Further Topics

- Event evaluation-based approaches (OCC model and appraisals)
- Emotion role labeling and stimulus/cause detection
- Open challenges in emotion analysis
- Ethical Considerations

5 Reading List

Although no particular prior knowledge is necessary for attending the tutorial, we recommend the attendees which are new to the emotion analysis to read the following works from the references section:

- Peter J. Lang. 2010. Emotion and motivation: Toward consensus definitions and a common research purpose. Emotion review 2, 3:229–233.
- Robert Plutchik. 2001. The nature of emotions: Human emotions have deep evolutionary roots, a fact that may explain their complexity and provide tools for clinical practice. American scientist 89, 4:344–350.
- Laura Ana Maria Bostan and Roman Klinger. 2018. An analysis of annotated corpora for emotion classification in text. In Proceedings of the 27th International Conference on Computational Linguistics, pages 2104–2119.
- Emily Öhman, Marc Pàmies, Kaisla Kajava, and Jörg Tiedemann. 2020. XED: A multilingual dataset for sentiment analysis and emotion detection. In Proceedings of the 28th International Conference on Computational Linguistics, pages 6542–6552.
- Enrica Troiano, Laura Oberländer, and Roman Klinger. 2023. Dimensional modeling of emotions in text with appraisal theories: Corpus creation, annotation reliability, and prediction. Computational Linguistics, 49(1).

6 Instructors' Research Interests and Areas of Expertise

Sanja Štajner has over 14 years of research experience across academia and industry on various psycholinguistic topics in NLP. The last four years, she has led and participated in industry-oriented projects that combined psychology and NLP focusing on sentiment analysis, emotion detection, personality modelling, and mental health assessment. Sanja served as a COLING 2018 area chair for psycholinguistics and cognitive modelling track, and an ACL 2022 demo chair. She has experience as tutorial presenter (COLING 2018, AIST 2018, RANLP 2017) for international audiences and as a lecturer at Masters and PhD levels.

Roman Klinger is senior lecturer at Stuttgart University, where he teaches courses on Emotion Analysis since 2016 (see `https://www.emotionanalysis.de/`). He has been principal investigator on several externally funded projects with focus on emotion analysis. Roman served as senior area chair for sentiment analysis and argumentation mining at ACL 2022 and EACL 2021 and for evaluation and resources at EACL 2023. He was organizer of the WASSA workshop (on Computational Approaches to Subjectivity, Sentiment and Social Media Analysis) in 2018, 2019, 2022, and 2023.

7 Tutorial Materials

All tutorial materials will be made publicly available at: `eacl2023tutorial.github.io`.

8 Ethics Statement

One of the main goals of the tutorial is to raise awareness about open challenges in emotion analysis which can lead to possible unintended harms and ethical issues with models commonly used for emotion analysis in real-world applications.

Acknowledgements

Roman Klinger's work is partially funded by the German Research Council (DFG), project "Computational Event Analysis based on Appraisal Theories for Emotion Analysis" (CEAT, project number KL 2869/1-2).

References

Francisca Adoma Acheampong, Chen Wenyu, and Henry Nunoo-Mensah. 2020. Text-based emotion detection: Advances, challenges, and opportunities. *Engineering Reports*.

Cecilia Ovesdotter Alm, Dan Roth, and Richard Sproat. 2005. Emotions from text: Machine learning for text-based emotion prediction. In *Proceedings of Human Language Technology Conference and Conference on Empirical Methods in Natural Language Processing*, pages 579–586, Vancouver, British Columbia, Canada. Association for Computational Linguistics.

Laura Ana Maria Bostan, Evgeny Kim, and Roman Klinger. 2020. GoodNewsEveryone: A corpus of news headlines annotated with emotions, semantic roles, and reader perception. In *Proceedings of the 12th Language Resources and Evaluation Conference*, pages 1554–1566, Marseille, France.

Laura Ana Maria Bostan and Roman Klinger. 2018. An analysis of annotated corpora for emotion classification in text. In *Proceedings of the 27th International Conference on Computational Linguistics*, pages 2104–2119, Santa Fe, New Mexico, USA.

Joel Brynielsson, Fredrik Johansson, Carl Jonsson, and Anders Westling. 2014. Emotion classification of social media posts for estimating people's reactions to communicated alert messages during crises. *Secur. Informatics*, 3(1):7.

Sven Buechel and Udo Hahn. 2017. Readers vs. writers vs. texts: Coping with different perspectives of text understanding in emotion annotation. In *Proceedings of the 11th Linguistic Annotation Workshop*, pages 1–12, Valencia, Spain. Association for Computational Linguistics.

Dorottya Demszky, Dana Movshovitz-Attias, Jeongwoo Ko, Alan Cowen, Gaurav Nemade, and Sujith Ravi. 2020. GoEmotions: A dataset of fine-grained emotions. In *Proceedings of the 58th Annual Meeting of the Association for Computational Linguistics*, pages 4040–4054, Online. Association for Computational Linguistics.

Mandar Deshpande and Vignesh Rao. 2017. Depression detection using emotion artificial intelligence. In *2017 International Conference on Intelligent Sustainable Systems (ICISS)*, pages 858–862.

Bart Desmet and Véronique Hoste. 2013. Emotion detection in suicide notes. *Expert Systems with Applications*, 40(16):6351–6358.

Paul Ekman and Wallace V. Friesen. 1981. *The Repertoire of Nonverbal Behavior: Categories, Origins, Usage, and Coding*, pages 57–106. De Gruyter Mouton, Berlin, Boston.

Senait Gebremichael Tesfagergish, Jurgita Kapočiūtė-Dzikienė, and Robertas Damaševičius. 2022. Zero-shot emotion detection for semi-supervised sentiment analysis using sentence transformers and ensemble learning. *Applied Sciences*, 12:8662.

Gaël Guibon, Matthieu Labeau, Hélène Flamein, Luce Lefeuvre, and Chloé Clavel. 2021. Few-shot emotion recognition in conversation with sequential prototypical networks. In *Proceedings of the 2021 Conference on Empirical Methods in Natural Language Processing*, pages 6858–6870, Online and Punta Cana, Dominican Republic.

Chao-Chun Hsu, Sheng-Yeh Chen, Chuan-Chun Kuo, Ting-Hao Huang, and Lun-Wei Ku. 2018. EmotionLines: An emotion corpus of multi-party conversations. In *Proceedings of the Eleventh International*

Conference on Language Resources and Evaluation (LREC 2018), Miyazaki, Japan.

Pere-Lluís Huguet Cabot, David Abadi, Agneta Fischer, and Ekaterina Shutova. 2021. Us vs. them: A dataset of populist attitudes, news bias and emotions. In *Proceedings of the 16th Conference of the European Chapter of the Association for Computational Linguistics: Main Volume*, pages 1921–1945, Online.

Peter J. Lang. 2010. Emotion and motivation: Toward consensus definitions and a common research purpose. *Emotion review 2*, 3:229–233.

Yanran Li, Hui Su, Xiaoyu Shen, Wenjie Li, Ziqiang Cao, and Shuzi Niu. 2017. DailyDialog: A manually labelled multi-turn dialogue dataset. In *Proceedings of the Eighth International Joint Conference on Natural Language Processing (Volume 1: Long Papers)*, pages 986–995, Taipei, Taiwan. Asian Federation of Natural Language Processing.

Zhaojiang Lin, Andrea Madotto, Jamin Shin, Peng Xu, and Pascale Fung. 2019a. Moel: Mixture of empathetic listeners. *CoRR*, abs/1908.07687.

Zhaojiang Lin, Peng Xu, Genta Indra Winata, Zihan Liu, and Pascale Fung. 2019b. Caire: An end-to-end empathetic chatbot. *CoRR*, abs/1907.12108.

Maria L. Loureiro and Maria Alló. 2020. Sensing climate change and energy issues: Sentiment and emotion analysis with social media in the u.k. and spain. *Energy Policy*, 143:111490.

Yukun Ma, Khanh Linh Nguyen, Frank Z. Xing, and Erik Cambria. 2020. A survey on empathetic dialogue systems. *Information Fusion*, 64:50–70.

Saif Mohammad. 2012. #emotional tweets. In **SEM 2012: The First Joint Conference on Lexical and Computational Semantics – Volume 1: Proceedings of the main conference and the shared task, and Volume 2: Proceedings of the Sixth International Workshop on Semantic Evaluation (SemEval 2012)*, pages 246–255, Montréal, Canada. Association for Computational Linguistics.

Saif M. Mohammad, Xiao-Dan Zhu, Svetlana Kiritchenko, and Joel D. Martin. 2015. Sentiment, emotion, purpose, and style in electoral tweets. *Information Processing and Management*, 51:480–499.

Alena Neviarouskaya, Helmut Prendinger, and Mitsuru Ishizuka. 2010. @AM: Textual attitude analysis model. In *Proceedings of the NAACL HLT 2010 Workshop on Computational Approaches to Analysis and Generation of Emotion in Text*, pages 80–88, Los Angeles, CA.

Emily Öhman, Marc Pàmies, Kaisla Kajava, and Jörg Tiedemann. 2020. XED: A multilingual dataset for sentiment analysis and emotion detection. In *Proceedings of the 28th International Conference on Computational Linguistics*, pages 6542–6552, Barcelona, Spain (Online). International Committee on Computational Linguistics.

Ana Paiva, Iolanda Leite, Hana Boukricha, and Ipke Wachsmuth. 2017. Empathy in virtual agents and robots: A survey. *ACM Transactions on Interactive Intelligent Systems*, 7(3).

John P. Pestian, Pawel Matykiewicz, Michelle Linngust, Brett South, Ozlem Uzuner, Jan Wiebe, Kevin Bretonnel Cohen, John Hurdle, and Christopher Brew. 2012. Sentiment analysis of suicide notes: A shared task. *Biomedical Informatics Insights*, 5:3–16.

Flor Miriam Plaza-del Arco, María-Teresa Martín-Valdivia, and Roman Klinger. 2022. Natural language inference prompts for zero-shot emotion classification in text across corpora. In *Proceedings of the 29th International Conference on Computational Linguistics*, pages 6805–6817, Gyeongju, Republic of Korea.

Robert Plutchik. 1982. A psychoevolutionary theory of emotions. *Social Science Information 21*, pages 529–553.

Robert Plutchik. 2001. The nature of emotions: Human emotions have deep evolutionary roots, a fact that may explain their complexity and provide tools for clinical practice. *American scientist 89*, 4:344–350.

Hannah Rashkin, Eric Michael Smith, Margaret Li, and Y-Lan Boureau. 2019. Towards empathetic open-domain conversation models: A new benchmark and dataset. In *Proceedings of the 57th Annual Meeting of the Association for Computational Linguistics*, pages 5370–5381, Florence, Italy. Association for Computational Linguistics.

K. R. Scherer and H. G. Wallbott. 1994. Evidence for universality and cultural variation of differential emotion response patterning. *Journal of personality and social psychology*, 66 2:310–28.

Hendrik Schuff, Jeremy Barnes, Julian Mohme, Sebastian Padó, and Roman Klinger. 2017. Annotation, modelling and analysis of fine-grained emotions on a stance and sentiment detection corpus. In *Proceedings of the 8th Workshop on Computational Approaches to Subjectivity, Sentiment and Social Media Analysis*, pages 13–23, Copenhagen, Denmark. Association for Computational Linguistics.

N. Shanthi, Albert Alexander Stonier, Anli Sherine, T. Devaraju, S. Abinash, R. Ajay, V. Arul Prasath, and Vivekananda Ganji. 2022. An integrated approach for mental health assessment using emotion analysis and scales. *Healthcare Technology Letters*, n/a(n/a).

Jamin Shin, Peng Xu, Andrea Madotto, and Pascale Fung. 2019. Happybot: Generating empathetic dialogue responses by improving user experience lookahead. *CoRR*, abs/1906.08487.

Satish Mahadevan Srinivasan, Raghvinder S. Sangwan, Colin J. Neill, and Tianhai Zu. 2019. Power of predictive analytics: Using emotion classification of twitter data for predicting 2016 us presidential elections. *Social media and society*, 8:211–230.

Carlo Strapparava and Rada Mihalcea. 2007. SemEval-2007 task 14: Affective text. In *Proceedings of the Fourth International Workshop on Semantic Evaluations (SemEval-2007)*, pages 70–74, Prague, Czech Republic.

Martin Sykora, Suzanne Elayan, Ian R. Hodgkinson, Thomas W. Jackson, and Andrew West. 2022. The power of emotions: Leveraging user generated content for customer experience management. *Journal of Business Research*, 144:997–1006.

Enrica Troiano, Laura Oberländer, and Roman Klinger. 2023. Dimensional modeling of emotions in text with appraisal theories: Corpus creation, annotation reliability, and prediction. *Computational Linguistics*, 49(1).

Enrica Troiano, Sebastian Padó, and Roman Klinger. 2019. Crowdsourcing and validating event-focused emotion corpora for German and English. In *Proceedings of the 57th Annual Meeting of the Association for Computational Linguistics*, pages 4005–4011, Florence, Italy. Association for Computational Linguistics.

Sanja Štajner. 2021. Exploring Reliability of Gold Labels for Emotion Detection in Twitter. In *Proceedings of the 13th international conference on Recent Advances in Natural Language Processing (RANLP)*, pages 1350–1359.

Qiping Wang, Tingxuan Su, Raymond Yiu Keung Lau, and Haoran Xie. 2023. Deepemotionnet: Emotion mining for corporate performance analysis and prediction. *Information Processing & Management*, 60(3):103151.

Summarization of Dialogues and Conversations At Scale

Diyi Yang
Computer Science Department
Stanford University
diyiy@stanford.edu

Chenguang Zhu
Microsoft Azure Cognitive
Services Research
chezhu@microsoft.com

1 Introduction

Conversations are the natural communication format for people. This fact has motivated the large body of question answering and chatbot research as a seamless way for people to interact with machines. The conversations between people however, captured as video, audio or private or public written conversations, largely remain untapped as a source of compelling starting point for developing language technology. Summarizing such conversations can be enormously beneficial: automatic minutes for meetings or meeting highlights sent to relevant people can optimize communication in various groups while minimizing demands on people's time; similarly analysis of conversations in online support groups can provide valuable information to doctors about the patient concerns.

Summarizing written and spoken conversation poses unique research challenges—text reformulation, discourse and meaning analysis beyond the sentence, collecting data, and proper evaluation metrics. All these have been revisited by researchers since the emergence of neural approaches as the dominant approach for solving language processing problems. In this tutorial, we will survey the cutting-edge methods for summarization of conversations, covering key sub-areas whose combination is needed for a successful solution.

2 Tutorial Outline

This will be a **three-hour** tutorial devoted to the **cutting-edge** topic of conversation summarization. Our tutorial will include three sessions. Each session will be 40 minutes, followed by 10 minutes for Q&A and 10 minutes for a break. Each part includes an overview of the corresponding topic and widely used methods and a deep dive into representative research. The detailed tutorial schedule can be found in Table 1.

Slot	Theme
Session 1: Introduction to Conversation Summarization	
14:15 – 14:20	Tutorial presenters introduction
14:20 – 14:35	Introduce the task, its history and impact
14:35 – 15:15	Compare document and conversation summarization (CS), and datasets
15:15 – 15:30	Coffee Break
Session 2: Pretraining and Methods	
15:30 – 15:50	Pretraining in Conversation summarization
15:50 – 16:30	Classic models in summarizing conversations, dialogue, and meetings
16:30 – 16:45	Coffee Break
Session 3: Evaluation and Challenges	
16:45 – 17:00	Structures and knowledge to improve conversation summarization
17:00 – 17:30	Evaluation metrics and issues
17:30 – 17:45	Open questions and challenges
17:45 – 18:00	Conclusion

Table 1: Tutorial schedule.

2.1 Introduction

Compared to summarizing news reports or encyclopedia articles, summarizing conversations—an essential part of human-human/machine interaction where most important pieces of information are scattered across various utterances of different speakers—remains relatively under-investigated. Yet capabilities for automatic dialog summarization hold the promise to facilitate information access, especially in corporate (or large group) settings. For instance, participants in corporate meetings usually want to get high-level synopsis of the meeting content and action items to review after meeting. People who miss the meeting also want to quickly get the main topics discussed in the meeting. Another scenario is customer service, where customer calls with the agents can be summarized, categorized and analyzed. This can help agents to find frequent problems to answer, product issues to follow, etc. in order to improve service quality.

Proceedings of the 17th Conference of the European Chapter of the Association for Computational Linguistics
Tutorial Abstracts, pages 13–18

2.1.1 Datasets

Text summarization was dominated by unsupervised methods for decades (Nenkova and McKeown, 2011, 2012), due to the lack of suitable size datasets for the task. The field has been transformed by the introduction of large-scale datasets such as CNN/DailyMail (Hermann et al., 2015) and XSUM (Narayan et al., 2018). The past decade also saw the emergence of many dialogue and conversation datasets such as MultiWoz (Budzianowski et al., 2018) and Ubuntu (Lowe et al., 2015). However, the progress in datasets for conversation summarization is comparatively limited. Existing public datasets in this field are either small in scale or limited to a specific domain. We argue that there are two main reasons. First, unlike news articles, conversations usually happen in relatively private environment, which raises privacy concerns for release of public datasets. Secondly, a conversation is typically quite long, and the conversation participants often have different standpoints and language styles with frequent topic changes. These all propose great challenges for labelers to produce accurate summaries as ground-truth labels.

Despite these difficulties, new research datasets for conversation summarization have been developed recently. For instance, SAMSum (Gliwa et al., 2019a) hires linguists to write summaries for 16,369 messenger-like open-domain daily conversations. MediaSum (Zhu et al., 2021) leverages public transcripts with overviews and topic descriptions from CNN and NPR to produce 463.6K dialogues with summaries. DialogSum (Chen et al., 2021) hires annotators to write summaries for 13,460 dialogues from several public dialogue corpora. The CovoSumm dataset (Fabbri et al., 2021) provides 250 development and 250 test summaries for dialogs from broad domains covering news article comments, discussion forms and debates, community question answering, and email threads. QMSum (Zhong et al., 2021b) consists of 1,808 query-summary pairs over 232 meetings. We will provide a systematic review of these newly released resources.

2.2 Methods

2.2.1 Pretraining

Pre-trained language representations are at the core of most NLP technologies (Devlin et al., 2018; Radford et al., 2018; Liu et al., 2019b). They provide representations that capture language meaning from large amount of data, easily tunable for specific downstream tasks. For instance, the super language models with hundreds of billions of parameters, e.g., GPT-3 (Brown et al., 2020), PaLM (Chowdhery et al., 2022) and OPT (Zhang et al., 2022), have demonstrated strong capabilities in many different tasks, including dialogue summarization.

These foundation models are typically trained on web corpus, comprising mostly of articles and monologues, partly because of their general availability and partly because conversational online exchanges often contain more problematic stereotypes. However, matching pre-training data to downstream tasks—both in the type of textual data and the self-supervised objective for pretraining—is important for performance in downstream tasks. Motivated by this, several pre-trained dialogue models have been proposed for conversation summarization (Feng et al., 2021). These methods pre-train the model with self-supervised tasks, such as recovering altered conversation turns, predicting speakers, reordering shuffled turns, predicting masked utterances in the conversation. These tasks only require unlabeled conversation corpus, i.e., no labeled summary is needed, which greatly expands the availability of data that can be used to improve the quality of pre-trained models. It has been shown that after such pre-training on conversation corpus, the performance on downstream conversational summarization tasks can be greatly improved.

For instance, DialogLM (Zhong et al., 2021a) continues to pre-train the UniLMv2 (Bao et al., 2020) model with several window-based denoising tasks such as recovering the conversation text after randomly reshuffling the turns. The pre-training leads to considerable improvement on both conversation understanding and summarization tasks. HMNet (Zhu et al., 2020a) takes a different approach by creating pseudo meetings from news summarization datasets. The model is trained to produce the summary which is the concatenation of the 4 news articles' summaries. Experiments show that the pre-training can increase the ROUGE-1 metric on AMI (McCowan et al., 2005) and ICSI (Janin et al., 2003) by 4~5 points.

We will overview pretraining methods specific to dialog summarization and will sythesize the impact of data and objectives on downstream tasks across the published literature.

2.2.2 Abstractive Summarization Models

Unlike news, conversations can rarely be summarized meaningfully with extractive approaches. Abstractive summarization is the default expectation for dialogues. Other than directly applying document summarization models to conversational settings (Gliwa et al., 2019b), models tailored for conversation are designed to achieve the state-of-the-art performances such as modeling conversations in a hierarchical way (Zhao et al., 2019; Zhu et al., 2020b). The rich structured information in conversations are also explored and leveraged such as dialogue acts (Goo and Chen, 2018), key point/entity sequences (Liu et al., 2019a; Narayan et al., 2021), topic segments (Liu et al., 2019c; Li et al., 2019), stage developments (Chen and Yang, 2020), discourse relations (Chen and Yang, 2021b; Feng et al., 2020a). Recent work has also explicitly models coreference information to deal with the complex coreference phenomenon in dialogues (Liu et al., 2021). External information like commonsense knowledge has also been incorporated to help understand the global conversation context as well (Feng et al., 2020b).

We will cover how classic statistical models are used to summarize dialogues and multi-party meetings, as well as the recent techniques in using large pretrained language models and diverse neural architectures that take into account conversation characteristics. We will also go through and discuss how to evaluate dialogue summarization models, ranging from classical ROUGE to the recent automatic metrics like BERTScore, as well as multiple widely used qualitative measures.

2.3 Open Questions

We will conclude the tutorial with a discussion of more exploratory work around the actual usability of summarization approaches. For example, naturally occurring conversations are long, so segmentation and representations for long text become necessary. Processing time and processing cost for many of the methods is high, both because of the complexity of analyzing discourse and topics and because of the length of the input. We will conclude the section by covering estimates of costs for conversation summarization.

We will cover a discussion on robustness of methods, i.e. their ability to generalize across datasets rather than needing finetuning for each dataset. Finetuning different versions of the model for each dataset is not practical, as maintaining and deploying different fine-tuned versions is less realistic to be done in practice.

Finally, we will discuss scenarios for user evaluation of conversation summarization technology. Such extrinsic evaluations would be needed to move the technology from the realm of research to technological reality. We will include a short segement in which tutorial participants will brainstorm study designs, to validate specific claims about the utility of summarization models.

We will also discuss potential biases and ethical issues related to conversation summarization. This last part of the tutorial is meant to introduce open research questions, so that newcomers to the field of conversation summarization can be equipped to make their own contributions in some of the areas of open questions.

3 Tutorial Presenters

Diyi Yang is an assistant professor in the Computer Science Department at Stanford University. Her research focuses on dialogue summarization, learning with limited and noisy text data, user-centric language generation, and computational social science. Diyi has organized four workshops at NLP conferences: Widening NLP Workshops at NAACL 2018 and ACL 2019, Casual Inference workshop at EMNLP 2021, and NLG Evaluation workshop at EMNLP 2021. She also gave a tutorial at ACL 2022 on Learning with Limited Data.

Chenguang Zhu is a Principal Research Manager in Microsoft Azure Cognitive Services Research Group, where he leads the Knowledge & Language Team. His research in NLP covers text summarization, task-oriented dialogue and knowledge graph,. Dr. Zhu has led teams to achieve first places in multiple NLP competitions. He holds a Ph.D. degree in Computer Science from Stanford University. Dr. Zhu has given talks at Stanford University, Carnegie Mellon University and UC Berkeley. He has given tutorials on Knowledge-Augmented Methods for Natural Language Processing at ACL 2022 and WSDM 2023. He is also the main organizer of The Workshop on Knowledge Augmented Methods for NLP at AAAI 2023.

4 Diversity Considerations

The conversation summarization techniques we introduce is language agnostic. Thus, they can be applied to data in various languages and localities with some extent of adaption. Code-switch and multilingual models for conversation summarization can scale this work beyond English.

Our presenter team will share our tutorial with a worldwide audience by promoting it on social media. Our presenters span over junior (Diyi Yang) and senior researchers (Chenguang Zhu) with a female. Diyi is from academia and Chenguang is from industry. Thus, we have diversified instructors which will also help encourage diverse audience. Diyi has experience co-organizing Widening NLP Workshops at both NAACL and ACL, and actively works on inviting undergraduate students to research and promoting diversity such as by speaking at AI4ALL and local high-schools at Atlanta. We will work with ACL/NAACL D&I teams, and consult resources such as the BIG directory to diversify our audience participation.

5 Reading List and Prerequisite

5.1 Prerequisite

The prerequisite includes familiarity with basic machine learning and deep learning models, especially those typically used in modern NLP for summarization, including sequence to sequence learning, transformers, etc. Furthermore, this tutorial assumes background in basic probability, linear algebra, and calculus. We will also provide introduction materials and additional readings.

Reading List

1. Samsum corpus: A human-annotated dialogue dataset for abstractive summarization (Gliwa et al., 2019c)

2. A Hierarchical network for abstractive meeting summarization with cross-domain pretraining (Zhu et al., 2020a)

3. Dialoglm: Pre-trainedmodel for long dialogue understanding and summa-rization (Zhong et al., 2021a)

4. Multi-View Sequence-to-Sequence Models with Conversational Structure for Abstractive Dialogue Summarization (Chen and Yang, 2020)

5. Simple Conversational Data Augmentation for Semi-supervised Abstractive Dialogue Summarization (Chen and Yang, 2021a)

6. QMSum: A New Benchmark for Query-based Multi-domain Meeting Summarization (Zhong et al., 2021b)

7. ConvoSumm: Conversation Summarization Benchmark and Improved Abstractive Summarization with Argument Mining (Fabbri et al., 2021)

5.2 Breadth

While we will give pointers to dozens of relevant papers over the course of the tutorial, we plan to cover around 7-8 research papers in close detail. Only 1-2 of the "deep dive" papers will come from the presenter team.

6 Tutorial Details

6.1 Audience Size

We expect the audience size to be around 100 for a physical conference, and around 150 for a virtual conference. Our tutorial will likely bring a similar audience as the SummDial: A SIGDial 2021 Special Session on Summarization of Dialogues and Multi-Party Meetings `https://elitr.github.io/automatic-minuting/summdial.html`.

6.2 Preferable venues

ACL-IJCNLP, EMNLP and EACL would be preferable, as they would fit better with the organizers' schedules and our tutorial's emphasis on machine learning. We would like to have access to Gather.Town for interactive Q&A for the online portion of the tutorial.

6.3 Open Access

We will put the slides, code, and other teaching materials online for public access, as well as consent to adding the video recording of our tutorial in the ACL Anthology.

7 Ethics Statement

Certain conversation data might come from private dialogues between people. Thus, privacy considerations must be take to ensure all data that is released conforms to regulations and are under consent. As conversations and large-pretrained language models may have bias in various forms, summarization models may contain the same form of bias and should be reviewed and modified if necessary.

References

Hangbo Bao, Li Dong, Furu Wei, Wenhui Wang, Nan Yang, Xiaodong Liu, Yu Wang, Jianfeng Gao, Songhao Piao, Ming Zhou, et al. 2020. Unilmv2: Pseudo-masked language models for unified language model pre-training. In *International Conference on Machine Learning*, pages 642–652. PMLR.

Tom Brown, Benjamin Mann, Nick Ryder, Melanie Subbiah, Jared D Kaplan, Prafulla Dhariwal, Arvind Neelakantan, Pranav Shyam, Girish Sastry, Amanda Askell, et al. 2020. Language models are few-shot learners. *Advances in neural information processing systems*, 33:1877–1901.

Paweł Budzianowski, Tsung-Hsien Wen, Bo-Hsiang Tseng, Inigo Casanueva, Stefan Ultes, Osman Ramadan, and Milica Gašić. 2018. Multiwoz-a large-scale multi-domain wizard-of-oz dataset for task-oriented dialogue modelling. *arXiv preprint arXiv:1810.00278*.

Jiaao Chen and Diyi Yang. 2020. Multi-view sequence-to-sequence models with conversational structure for abstractive dialogue summarization. In *Proceedings of the 2020 Conference on Empirical Methods in Natural Language Processing (EMNLP)*, pages 4106–4118.

Jiaao Chen and Diyi Yang. 2021a. Simple conversational data augmentation for semi-supervised abstractive conversation summarization.

Jiaao Chen and Diyi Yang. 2021b. Structure-aware abstractive conversation summarization via discourse and action graphs. In *Proceedings of the 2021 Conference of the North American Chapter of the Association for Computational Linguistics: Human Language Technologies*, pages 1380–1391, Online. Association for Computational Linguistics.

Yulong Chen, Yang Liu, and Yue Zhang. 2021. Dialogsum challenge: Summarizing real-life scenario dialogues. In *Proceedings of the 14th International Conference on Natural Language Generation*, pages 308–313.

Aakanksha Chowdhery, Sharan Narang, Jacob Devlin, Maarten Bosma, Gaurav Mishra, Adam Roberts, Paul Barham, Hyung Won Chung, Charles Sutton, Sebastian Gehrmann, et al. 2022. Palm: Scaling language modeling with pathways. *arXiv preprint arXiv:2204.02311*.

Jacob Devlin, Ming-Wei Chang, Kenton Lee, and Kristina Toutanova. 2018. Bert: Pre-training of deep bidirectional transformers for language understanding. *arXiv preprint arXiv:1810.04805*.

Alexander Fabbri, Faiaz Rahman, Imad Rizvi, Borui Wang, Haoran Li, Yashar Mehdad, and Dragomir Radev. 2021. ConvoSumm: Conversation summarization benchmark and improved abstractive summarization with argument mining. In *Proceedings of the 59th Annual Meeting of the Association for Computational Linguistics and the 11th International Joint Conference on Natural Language Processing (Volume 1: Long Papers)*, pages 6866–6880, Online. Association for Computational Linguistics.

Xiachong Feng, Xiaocheng Feng, and Bing Qin. 2021. A survey on dialogue summarization: Recent advances and new frontiers. *arXiv preprint arXiv:2107.03175*.

Xiachong Feng, Xiaocheng Feng, Bing Qin, Xinwei Geng, and Ting Liu. 2020a. Dialogue discourse-aware graph convolutional networks for abstractive meeting summarization.

Xiachong Feng, Xiaocheng Feng, Bing Qin, and Ting Liu. 2020b. Incorporating commonsense knowledge into abstractive dialogue summarization via heterogeneous graph networks. *arXiv preprint arXiv:2010.10044*.

Bogdan Gliwa, Iwona Mochol, Maciej Biesek, and Aleksander Wawer. 2019a. Samsum corpus: A human-annotated dialogue dataset for abstractive summarization. *arXiv preprint arXiv:1911.12237*.

Bogdan Gliwa, Iwona Mochol, Maciej Biesek, and Aleksander Wawer. 2019b. SAMSum corpus: A human-annotated dialogue dataset for abstractive summarization. In *Proceedings of the 2nd Workshop on New Frontiers in Summarization*, pages 70–79, Hong Kong, China. Association for Computational Linguistics.

Bogdan Gliwa, Iwona Mochol, Maciej Biesek, and Aleksander Wawer. 2019c. Samsum corpus: A human-annotated dialogue dataset for abstractive summarization. *EMNLP-IJCNLP 2019*, page 70.

Chih-Wen Goo and Yun-Nung Chen. 2018. Abstractive dialogue summarization with sentence-gated modeling optimized by dialogue acts. *2018 IEEE Spoken Language Technology Workshop (SLT)*.

Karl Moritz Hermann, Tomas Kocisky, Edward Grefenstette, Lasse Espeholt, Will Kay, Mustafa Suleyman, and Phil Blunsom. 2015. Teaching machines to read and comprehend. *Advances in neural information processing systems*, pages 1693–1701.

Adam Janin, Don Baron, Jane Edwards, Dan Ellis, David Gelbart, Nelson Morgan, Barbara Peskin, Thilo Pfau, Elizabeth Shriberg, Andreas Stolcke, et al. 2003. The icsi meeting corpus. *2003 IEEE International Conference on Acoustics, Speech, and Signal Processing, 2003. Proceedings.(ICASSP'03)*, 1:I–I.

Manling Li, Lingyu Zhang, Heng Ji, and Richard J. Radke. 2019. Keep meeting summaries on topic: Abstractive multi-modal meeting summarization. In *Proceedings of the 57th Annual Meeting of the Association for Computational Linguistics*, pages 2190–2196, Florence, Italy. Association for Computational Linguistics.

Chunyi Liu, Peng Wang, Jiang Xu, Zang Li, and Jieping Ye. 2019a. Automatic dialogue summary generation for customer service. In *Proceedings of the 25th ACM SIGKDD International Conference on Knowledge Discovery & Data Mining*, KDD19, page 1957–1965, New York, NY, USA. Association for Computing Machinery.

Yinhan Liu, Myle Ott, Naman Goyal, Jingfei Du, Mandar Joshi, Danqi Chen, Omer Levy, Mike Lewis, Luke Zettlemoyer, and Veselin Stoyanov. 2019b. Roberta: A robustly optimized bert pretraining approach. *arXiv preprint arXiv:1907.11692*.

Zhengyuan Liu, Angela Ng, Sheldon Lee, Ai Ti Aw, and Nancy F. Chen. 2019c. Topic-aware pointer-generator networks for summarizing spoken conversations. *2019 IEEE Automatic Speech Recognition and Understanding Workshop (ASRU)*.

Zhengyuan Liu, Ke Shi, and Nancy Chen. 2021. Coreference-aware dialogue summarization. In *Proceedings of the 22nd Annual Meeting of the Special Interest Group on Discourse and Dialogue*, pages 509–519, Singapore and Online. Association for Computational Linguistics.

Ryan Lowe, Nissan Pow, Iulian Serban, and Joelle Pineau. 2015. The ubuntu dialogue corpus: A large dataset for research in unstructured multi-turn dialogue systems. *arXiv preprint arXiv:1506.08909*.

Iain McCowan, Jean Carletta, Wessel Kraaij, Simone Ashby, S Bourban, M Flynn, M Guillemot, Thomas Hain, J Kadlec, Vasilis Karaiskos, et al. 2005. The ami meeting corpus. *Proceedings of the 5th International Conference on Methods and Techniques in Behavioral Research*, 88:100.

Shashi Narayan, Shay B Cohen, and Mirella Lapata. 2018. Don't give me the details, just the summary! topic-aware convolutional neural networks for extreme summarization. *arXiv preprint arXiv:1808.08745*.

Shashi Narayan, Yao Zhao, Joshua Maynez, Gonçalo Simoes, and Ryan McDonald. 2021. Planning with entity chains for abstractive summarization.

Ani Nenkova and Kathleen R. McKeown. 2011. Automatic summarization. *Found. Trends Inf. Retr.*, 5(2-3):103–233.

Ani Nenkova and Kathleen R. McKeown. 2012. A survey of text summarization techniques. In Charu C. Aggarwal and ChengXiang Zhai, editors, *Mining Text Data*, pages 43–76. Springer.

Alec Radford, Karthik Narasimhan, Tim Salimans, and Ilya Sutskever. 2018. Improving language understanding by generative pre-training.

Susan Zhang, Stephen Roller, Naman Goyal, Mikel Artetxe, Moya Chen, Shuohui Chen, Christopher Dewan, Mona Diab, Xian Li, Xi Victoria Lin, et al. 2022. Opt: Open pre-trained transformer language models. *arXiv preprint arXiv:2205.01068*.

Zhou Zhao, Haojie Pan, Changjie Fan, Yan Liu, Linlin Li, Min Yang, and Deng Cai. 2019. Abstractive meeting summarization via hierarchical adaptive segmental network learning. In *The World Wide Web Conference*, WWW '19, page 3455–3461, New York, NY, USA. Association for Computing Machinery.

Ming Zhong, Yang Liu, Yichong Xu, Chenguang Zhu, and Michael Zeng. 2021a. Dialoglm: Pre-trained model for long dialogue understanding and summarization. *arXiv preprint arXiv:2109.02492*.

Ming Zhong, Da Yin, Tao Yu, Ahmad Zaidi, Mutethia Mutuma, Rahul Jha, Ahmed Hassan Awadallah, Asli Celikyilmaz, Yang Liu, Xipeng Qiu, and Dragomir Radev. 2021b. QMSum: A new benchmark for query-based multi-domain meeting summarization. In *Proceedings of the 2021 Conference of the North American Chapter of the Association for Computational Linguistics: Human Language Technologies*, pages 5905–5921, Online. Association for Computational Linguistics.

Chenguang Zhu, Yang Liu, Jie Mei, and Michael Zeng. 2021. Mediasum: A large-scale media interview dataset for dialogue summarization. *arXiv preprint arXiv:2103.06410*.

Chenguang Zhu, Ruochen Xu, Michael Zeng, and Xuedong Huang. 2020a. A hierarchical network for abstractive meeting summarization with cross-domain pretraining. arXiv:2004.02016.

Chenguang Zhu, Ruochen Xu, Michael Zeng, and Xuedong Huang. 2020b. A hierarchical network for abstractive meeting summarization with cross-domain pretraining. In *Proceedings of the 2020 Conference on Empirical Methods in Natural Language Processing (EMNLP)*, Online. Association for Computational Linguistics.

Understanding Ethics in NLP Authoring and Reviewing

Luciana Benotti and **Karën Fort** and **Min-Yen Kan** and **Yulia Tsvetkov**
acl-ethics-committee@inria.fr

Abstract

With NLP research now quickly being transferred into real-world applications, it is important to be aware of and think through the consequences of our scientific investigation. Such ethical considerations are important in both authoring and reviewing. This tutorial will equip participants with basic guidelines for thinking deeply about ethical issues and review common considerations that recur in NLP research. The methodology is interactive and participatory, including case studies and working in groups. Importantly, the participants will be co-building the tutorial outcomes and will be working to create further tutorial materials to share as public outcomes.

1 Motivation and structure

In late 2021, the Association for Computational Linguistics' executive committee appointed an Ethics Committee to investigate long-term ethical issues of the community's research and legislate any policy and workflow changes to the authoring, reviewing and other processes. The committee surveyed the constituency's opinions, wants and needs, finding that the majority of respondents felt that clear guidelines on acceptable practices regarding authoring and reviewing were needed. Specifically, in response to the question "What do you think are the most urgent tasks for the global *CL ethics committee?", 50% of respondents highlighted the need for more resources and discussion forums to raise awareness in the community about ethical issues in research and to clarify ethical review policies, 36% specifically mentioned the importance of creating dedicated training materials for authors and reviewers, and 26% encouraged more outreach initiatives to facilitate discussion about ethical research in the community.

This tutorial proposal thus follows from the mandate from the survey, such that more interactive opportunities exist to best communicate and train our membership on ethical guidelines and research practices.

The tutorial also draws on related, successful past tutorials on NLP reviewing and socially responsible NLP ($\approx$100 participants) (Cohen et al., 2021; Tsvetkov et al., 2018), where some of the proposed tutorial instructors have been involved.

We propose a hybrid tutorial to best allow equitable access to the topic of this tutorial, especially to familiarize new community members and those who cannot afford access to attend physically. We plan to have dedicated presenters that can coordinate activities for the expected online participants. We may plan to use specific e-resources that can help facilitate virtual group discussions (e.g., Padlet, PollEverywhere, Google Docs, Slack).

We intend to make the tutorial presentation materials publicly available, in alignment with the stated goals of the tutorials. As an example, annotated presentation slides (with presenter notes) will be made available, such that tutorial participants can bring exercises of different lengths into classroom settings for research groups as well as undergraduate and graduate classes. We will organize a separate website via a Github repository[1] (to be owned by the ACL) to centralize our tutorial resources for long-term and public access.

However, due to the sensitive and formative nature of the small-group discussions, we will not record the small-group discussions so that participants can speak freely and off-the-record. The plenary, lecture-styled sessions (Sessions 1 and 7) may be recorded live, or pre-recorded offline.

This proposal tutorial aligns with the theme track "Reality Check"of ACL 2023. Most of the challenges addressed by the theme track, including out-of-domain generalization, adversarial attacks, spurious patterns (both linguistic and social), insensitivity to basic linguistic perturbations such as

[1] https://github.com/acl-org/ethics-tutorial, or similar (not yet published).

Proceedings of the 17th Conference of the European Chapter of the Association for Computational Linguistics
Tutorial Abstracts, pages 19–24

Segment Topic	Led by
1. Introduction and Foundations for Ethics	Presenters
2. Case Studies: Problematic Ethical Research — First reading	Participants
3. Structured Interaction / Dialogue	Presenters, Participants
4. Case studies — Second reading (Rotation)	Participants
5. Group Presentations	Group Leads
6. Summary and Common Issues	Presenters
7. Discussing and Troubleshooting Ethics and Further Resources	Presenters

Table 1: Tutorial Outline. Each segments' duration is ~30 minutes, but 3 hours in total. Segments 2–6 will be conducted in small-group interaction.

negation, sensitivity to perturbations that should not matter (e.g., order and wording of prompts), are deeply related to ethical considerations of NLP research. In particular, proper discussion of risks (e.g., failure modes and vulnerabilities to adversarial attacks) and limitations (the scope of your claims, not overselling) is an integral to the theme and also for ethics authoring and reviewing. Finally, the theme track raises the question "what is an improvement in the real-world?", which is directly related to the social impact issues addressed by ethics reviewing.

2 Tutorial Content

Type: 1/2 day, Introductory
Expected Attendees: 100
Audience: Authors and reviewers, interested parties
Desired Location: Preferably ACL (Toronto, Canada)
Prerequisites: Introductory background in natural language processing and deep learning, including a basic familiarity of commonly-used approaches to text classification and generation, and standard NLP tasks. Fluent command of English.

Ethical consideration overarch our duties as researchers and scientists. As members of our community, and representatives of our works to both the general public and practitioners, we need to consider the ramifications of our work. The need for a better understanding of ethics is reflected in both authoring and reviewing, key functions of our community's peer review process.

Unintended and harmful ethical lapses and consequences can be largely avoided through continuing communication. Rather than assume that research is purely an intellectual pursuit, our tutorial invites participants to consider ethics as an integral component of the holistic framework of impactful research work. Table 1 presents our proposed tutorial's outline. Our aim is to provide hands-on experience with ethical issues through a small-group activity, both at the physical conference and in breakout rooms for online participants.

Ethics requires healthy debate and deep thought, and for these reasons, our structure incorporates a Socratic exercise, where participants spend a large part of the session discussing a concrete case of problematic research. A Community of Inquiry[2] approach will be taken such that participants engage in role-playing and discussing about ethical issues through reading 1–2 problematic hypothetical research abstracts from a curated set (§ 2.1). Using Socratic-style questioning, presenters guide the participants to engender discussion and realise ethical issues in the works.

Importantly, the participants will be co-building the tutorial outcomes and will be working to create further tutorial materials to share as public outcomes of the exercises. For many issues in ethics, the evolving discussion creates more value than the actual conclusions. This is why we propose such a dialectic approach.

To encapsulate the exercise, the presenters will first introduce the key ways that ethics impacts authoring and reviewing (Segment 1), summarise the group discussions' key points (Segment 6) and conclude with pointers to references and other training materials (Segment 7), including best practices for authoring ethical consideration sections (Benotti and Blackburn, 2022) and reviewing.

Due to the necessary interactivity of the session, we plan to limit the registrations for the tutorial to 100. This is to cater to having approximately a 25:1 ratio for presenters to participants. A larger volume than this jeopardizes the necessary interactive nature of the tutorial, which requires input from all participants.

2.1 Case studies

In the interactive portion of the tutorial, we will discuss research abstracts and will facilitate group discussions guided by critical questions about the proposed technology. Participants will be encour-

[2] https://en.wikipedia.org/wiki/Community_of_inquiry

aged to discuss the following questions:

- Ethics of the research question: Would answering this research question advance science without violating social contracts? What are potentials for misuse?
- Social impact of the proposed technology and its potential dual use: Who could benefit from such a technology? Who can be harmed by such a technology? Could sharing data and models have major effects on people's lives?
- Privacy: Who owns the data? Understanding the differences between published versus publicized data, understanding the concept of user consent, and thinking about implicit assumptions of users on how their data will be used.
- Bias in data: What are possible artifacts in data, given population-specific distributions? How representative is this data to address the target task?
- Social bias and unfairness in models: Is there sufficient control for confounding variables and corner cases? Does the system optimize for the "right" objective? Could the system amplify data bias?
- Is the proposed evaluation sufficient? Is there a utility-based evaluation beyond accuracy; e.g., measurements of false positive and false negative rates as measurements of fairness? What is "the cost" of misclassification and fault (in)tolerance?

Our case studies will be hypothetical; i.e., we will not use abstracts from existing studies but will create abstracts that will allow us to highlight potential ethical issues covering multiple, diverse ethics-related topics, including human subjects research and institutional review board (IRB) approval, bias and fairness, privacy, misinformation, toxicity/content moderation, energy considerations/green AI. We will develop several representative case studies for participants to choose from; we show an example below that illustrates multiple problematic aspects within one study, which was adapted from an actual problematic recent study.

The following abstract introduces an unethical research question, a demographically biased data set, a data collection procedure that violates user privacy, a problematic evaluation procedure, and claims/potential applications that can lead to significant harms to individuals.

Abstract: Faces contain more information about sexual orientation than can be perceived by the human brain. We used deep neural networks to extract features from over 35 thousand facial images. Given a single facial image, a classifier could correctly distinguish between gay and heterosexual men in 80% of cases, and in 70% of cases for women. Accuracy increased to 90% and 80%, respectively, given five facial images per person. Facial features employed by the classifier included both fixed (e.g., nose shape) and transient facial features (e.g., grooming style). Consistent with the prenatal hormone theory of sexual orientation, gay men and women tended to have gender-atypical facial morphology, expression, and grooming styles. Prediction models aimed at gender alone detected with 55% and 53% accuracy for gay males and gay females, respectively. Such findings advance our understanding of the origins of sexual orientation and the limits of human perception. Given that organizations are using computer vision algorithms to detect people's intimate traits, our findings expose a threat to the privacy and safety of gay men and women.

2.2 Readings

We will cover a diversity of primary research on ethics, sourced beyond the presenters' own works, in the plenary sessions of the tutorial. Also, due to the abbreviated length of the 1/2-day format, our tutorial will cross reference sources from the list, rather than specifically require participants to do readings before the tutorial.

A full reading list of over 200 works has been cross-compiled by the full ACL Ethics Committee, sourced from university courses on NLP Ethics and related topics. The list available on Github[3]. The list can be updated by pull requests and is sortable by both topic and publication type. Topics and readings include the following among others: data usage (Drugan and Babych, 2010; Couillault et al., 2014; Mieskes, 2017; Bender and Friedman, 2018; Kann et al., 2019; Rogers et al., 2021; Gebru et al., 2021), crowdsourcing (Bederson and Quinn, 2011; Fort et al., 2011; Callison-Burch, 2014; Fort et al., 2014; Hara et al., 2018; Toxtli et al., 2021), biases (Blodgett et al., 2020), language diversity (Tatman, 2017; Jurgens et al., 2017; Zmigrod et al., 2019; Tan et al., 2020; Koenecke et al., 2020; Bird, 2020), rigorous and meaningful evaluation (Caglayan et al., 2020; Ethayarajh and Jurafsky, 2020; Antoniak and Mimno, 2021; Tan et al., 2021), environmental impact (Strubell et al., 2019; Zhou et al., 2020; Henderson et al.,

[3]https://github.com/acl-org/ethics-reading-list

2020; Schwartz et al., 2020; Bannour et al., 2021; Przybyła and Shardlow, 2022), and human harms and values (Winner, 1980; Hovy and Spruit, 2016; Leidner and Plachouras, 2017).

3 Presenters (listed in alphabetical order)

Luciana Benotti (*luciana.benotti@unc.edu.ar*, she/her) is an Associate Professor at the Universidad Nacional de Córdoba, in Argentina. Her research interests cover many aspects of situated and grounded language, including the study of misunderstandings, bias, stereotypes, and clarification requests. She is the elected chair of the NAACL executive board and is also serving as a member at large of the ACL Ethics committee.

Karën Fort (*karen.fort@sorbonne-universite.fr*, she/her) is an Associate Professor at Sorbonne Université and does her research at LORIA in Nancy, France. She has been working on ethics in NLP since 2014. She was co-chair of the first two ethics committees in the field (EMNLP 2020 and NAACL 2021) and is co-chair of the ACL ethics committee. She has been a member of the Sorbonne IRB between 2019 and 2022 and she teaches ethics at undergraduate and graduate level in Paris, Nancy, and the University of Malta.

Min-Yen Kan (*kanmy@comp.nus.edu.sg*, he/him): Associate Professor at the National University of Singapore and a co-chair of the ACL Ethics Committee. He has taught over 5,000 graduate and undergraduate students on his research interests in digital libraries, information retrieval and natural language processing.

Yulia Tsvetkov (*yuliats@cs.washington.edu*, she/her) is an Assistant Professor at the Paul G. Allen School of Computer Science and Engineering at the University of Washington, USA. Her research focuses on computational ethics, multilingual NLP, and machine learning for NLP. She developed a course on Computational Ethics in NLP and is teaching it at both undergraduate and graduate levels since 2017, and she is a co-chair of the ACL Ethics Committee.

4 Diversity considerations

The instructors of this tutorial are affiliated in different geographic regions. Luciana Benotti is in Latin America, Kären Fort in Europe, Min-Yen Kan in Asia and Yulia Tsvetkov in North America. Three of them identify with the female gender and one with the male gender. All of them are part of the ACL Ethics committee. We will promote this tutorial to all the ACL members but in particular to affinity groups such as Masakane, LatinX, North Africans, disabled in AI, indigenous in AI, Khipu and similar groups with the help of EquiCL. EquiCL is the only Big Interest Group in the ACL, its scope is equity and diversity and its current officers are Marine Carpuat (chair), Aline Villavicencio (secretary), Zeerak Waseem (communication with workshops and affinity groups). We think it is crucial to reach a diverse audience for this tutorial.

5 Ethical considerations

We are well aware that we do not compose a perfectly diverse committee and commit to pay close attention to ensure all participants' points of views are faithfully acknowledged.

We decided to use synthetic case studies in the form of abstracts, rather than real and complete articles, in order to preserve the anonymity of the authors, to refrain from personal criticism, and to allow the participants to focus more on the discussion than on the reading. We will create a variety of abstracts, with different forms, exemplifying different ethical issues, however, they will not cover all the possible ethical issues in the domain. Finally, the synthetic case studies will be clearly identified as such.

References

Maria Antoniak and David Mimno. 2021. Bad seeds: Evaluating lexical methods for bias measurement. In *Proceedings of the 59th Annual Meeting of the Association for Computational Linguistics and the 11th International Joint Conference on Natural Language Processing (Volume 1: Long Papers)*, pages 1889–1904, Online. Association for Computational Linguistics.

Nesrine Bannour, Sahar Ghannay, Aurélie Névéol, and Anne-Laure Ligozat. 2021. Evaluating the carbon footprint of NLP methods: a survey and analysis of existing tools. In *Proceedings of the Second Workshop on Simple and Efficient Natural Language Processing*, pages 11–21, Virtual. Association for Computational Linguistics.

Benjamin B. Bederson and Alexander J. Quinn. 2011. Web workers unite! addressing challenges of online laborers. In *CHI '11 Extended Abstracts on Human Factors in Computing Systems*, CHI EA '11, page 97–106, New York, NY, USA. Association for Computing Machinery.

Emily M. Bender and Batya Friedman. 2018. Data statements for natural language processing: Toward mitigating system bias and enabling better science. *Transactions of the Association for Computational Linguistics*, 6:587–604.

Luciana Benotti and Patrick Blackburn. 2022. Ethics consideration sections in natural language processing papers. To appear in *Proceedings of the 2022 Conference on Empirical Methods in Natural Language Processing*, Abu Dhabi, December 2022, Association for Computational Linguistics.

Steven Bird. 2020. Decolonising speech and language technology. In *Proceedings of the 28th International Conference on Computational Linguistics*, pages 3504–3519, Barcelona, Spain (Online). International Committee on Computational Linguistics.

Su Lin Blodgett, Solon Barocas, Hal Daumé III, and Hanna Wallach. 2020. Language (technology) is power: A critical survey of "bias" in NLP. In *Proceedings of the 58th Annual Meeting of the Association for Computational Linguistics*, pages 5454–5476, Online. Association for Computational Linguistics.

Ozan Caglayan, Pranava Madhyastha, and Lucia Specia. 2020. Curious case of language generation evaluation metrics: A cautionary tale. In *Proceedings of the 28th International Conference on Computational Linguistics*, pages 2322–2328, Barcelona, Spain (Online). International Committee on Computational Linguistics.

Chris Callison-Burch. 2014. Crowd-workers: Aggregating information across turkers to help them find higher paying work. *Proceedings of the AAAI Conference on Human Computation and Crowdsourcing*, 2(1):8–9.

Kevin Cohen, Karën Fort, Margot Mieskes, Aurélie Névéol, and Anna Rogers. 2021. Reviewing natural language processing research. In *Proceedings of the 16th Conference of the European Chapter of the Association for Computational Linguistics: Tutorial Abstracts*, pages 14–16, online. Association for Computational Linguistics.

Alain Couillault, Karën Fort, Gilles Adda, and Hugues de Mazancourt. 2014. Evaluating corpora documentation with regards to the ethics and big data charter. In *Proceedings of the Ninth International Conference on Language Resources and Evaluation (LREC'14)*, pages 4225–4229, Reykjavik, Iceland. European Language Resources Association (ELRA).

Jo Drugan and Bogdan Babych. 2010. Shared resources, shared values? ethical implications of sharing translation resources. In *Proceedings of the Second Joint EM+/CNGL Workshop: Bringing MT to the User: Research on Integrating MT in the Translation Industry*, pages 3–10, Denver, Colorado, USA. Association for Machine Translation in the Americas.

Kawin Ethayarajh and Dan Jurafsky. 2020. Utility is in the eye of the user: A critique of NLP leaderboards. In *Proceedings of the 2020 Conference on Empirical Methods in Natural Language Processing (EMNLP)*, pages 4846–4853, Online. Association for Computational Linguistics.

Karën Fort, Gilles Adda, and K. Bretonnel Cohen. 2011. Last words: Amazon Mechanical Turk: Gold mine or coal mine? *Computational Linguistics*, 37(2):413–420.

Karën Fort, Gilles Adda, Benoît Sagot, Joseph Mariani, and Alain Couillault. 2014. Crowdsourcing for language resource development: Criticisms about amazon mechanical turk overpowering use. In *Human Language Technology Challenges for Computer Science and Linguistics*, pages 303–314, Cham. Springer International Publishing.

Timnit Gebru, Jamie Morgenstern, Briana Vecchione, Jennifer Wortman Vaughan, Hanna Wallach, Hal Daumé III, and Kate Crawford. 2021. Datasheets for datasets. *Commun. ACM*, 64(12):86–92.

Kotaro Hara, Abigail Adams, Kristy Milland, Saiph Savage, Chris Callison-Burch, and Jeffrey P. Bigham. 2018. A data-driven analysis of workers' earnings on amazon mechanical turk. In *Proceedings of the 2018 CHI Conference on Human Factors in Computing Systems*, CHI '18, page 1–14, New York, NY, USA. Association for Computing Machinery.

Peter Henderson, Jieru Hu, Joshua Romoff, Emma Brunskill, Dan Jurafsky, and Joelle Pineau. 2020. Towards the systematic reporting of the energy and carbon footprints of machine learning. *Journal of Machine Learning Research*, 21(248):1–43.

Dirk Hovy and Shannon L. Spruit. 2016. The social impact of natural language processing. In *Proceedings of the 54th Annual Meeting of the Association for Computational Linguistics (Volume 2: Short Papers)*, pages 591–598, Berlin, Germany. Association for Computational Linguistics.

David Jurgens, Yulia Tsvetkov, and Dan Jurafsky. 2017. Incorporating dialectal variability for socially equitable language identification. In *Proceedings of the 55th Annual Meeting of the Association for Computational Linguistics (Volume 2: Short Papers)*, pages 51–57, Vancouver, Canada. Association for Computational Linguistics.

Katharina Kann, Kyunghyun Cho, and Samuel R. Bowman. 2019. Towards realistic practices in low-resource natural language processing: The development set. In *Proceedings of the 2019 Conference on Empirical Methods in Natural Language Processing and the 9th International Joint Conference on Natural Language Processing (EMNLP-IJCNLP)*, pages

3342–3349, Hong Kong, China. Association for Computational Linguistics.

Allison Koenecke, Andrew Nam, Emily Lake, Joe Nudell, Minnie Quartey, Zion Mengesha, Connor Toups, John R. Rickford, Dan Jurafsky, and Sharad Goel. 2020. Racial disparities in automated speech recognition. *Proceedings of the National Academy of Sciences*, 117(14):7684–7689.

Jochen L. Leidner and Vassilis Plachouras. 2017. Ethical by design: Ethics best practices for natural language processing. In *Proceedings of the First ACL Workshop on Ethics in Natural Language Processing*, pages 30–40, Valencia, Spain. Association for Computational Linguistics.

Margot Mieskes. 2017. A quantitative study of data in the NLP community. In *Proceedings of the First ACL Workshop on Ethics in Natural Language Processing*, pages 23–29, Valencia, Spain. Association for Computational Linguistics.

Piotr Przybyła and Matthew Shardlow. 2022. Using NLP to quantify the environmental cost and diversity benefits of in-person NLP conferences. In *Findings of the Association for Computational Linguistics: ACL 2022*, pages 3853–3863, Dublin, Ireland. Association for Computational Linguistics.

Anna Rogers, Timothy Baldwin, and Kobi Leins. 2021. 'just what do you think you're doing, dave?' a checklist for responsible data use in NLP. In *Findings of the Association for Computational Linguistics: EMNLP 2021*, pages 4821–4833, Punta Cana, Dominican Republic. Association for Computational Linguistics.

Roy Schwartz, Jesse Dodge, Noah A. Smith, and Oren Etzioni. 2020. Green ai. *Commun. ACM*, 63(12):54–63.

Emma Strubell, Ananya Ganesh, and Andrew McCallum. 2019. Energy and policy considerations for deep learning in NLP. In *Proceedings of the 57th Annual Meeting of the Association for Computational Linguistics*, pages 3645–3650, Florence, Italy. Association for Computational Linguistics.

Samson Tan, Shafiq Joty, Kathy Baxter, Araz Taeihagh, Gregory A. Bennett, and Min-Yen Kan. 2021. Reliability testing for natural language processing systems. In *Proceedings of the 59th Annual Meeting of the Association for Computational Linguistics and the 11th International Joint Conference on Natural Language Processing (Volume 1: Long Papers)*, pages 4153–4169, Online. Association for Computational Linguistics.

Samson Tan, Shafiq Joty, Lav Varshney, and Min-Yen Kan. 2020. Mind your inflections! Improving NLP for non-standard Englishes with Base-Inflection Encoding. In *Proceedings of the 2020 Conference on Empirical Methods in Natural Language Processing (EMNLP)*, pages 5647–5663, Online. Association for Computational Linguistics.

Rachael Tatman. 2017. Gender and dialect bias in YouTube's automatic captions. In *Proceedings of the First ACL Workshop on Ethics in Natural Language Processing*, pages 53–59, Valencia, Spain. Association for Computational Linguistics.

Carlos Toxtli, Siddharth Suri, and Saiph Savage. 2021. Quantifying the invisible labor in crowd work. *ACM Human Computer Interaction*, 5:1–26.

Yulia Tsvetkov, Vinodkumar Prabhakaran, and Rob Voigt. 2018. Socially responsible NLP. In *Proceedings of the 2018 Conference of the North American Chapter of the Association for Computational Linguistics: Tutorial Abstracts*, pages 24–26, New Orleans, Louisiana. Association for Computational Linguistics.

Langdon Winner. 1980. Do artifacts have politics? *Daedalus*, 109(1):121–136.

Sharon Zhou, Alexandra Luccioni, Gautier Cosne, Michael S Bernstein, and Yoshua Bengio. 2020. Establishing an evaluation metric to quantify climate change image realism. *Machine Learning: Science and Technology*, 1(2):025005.

Ran Zmigrod, Sabrina J. Mielke, Hanna Wallach, and Ryan Cotterell. 2019. Counterfactual data augmentation for mitigating gender stereotypes in languages with rich morphology. In *Proceedings of the 57th Annual Meeting of the Association for Computational Linguistics*, pages 1651–1661, Florence, Italy. Association for Computational Linguistics.

Tutorial: AutoML for NLP

Kevin Duh
Johns Hopkins University
Baltimore, USA
kevinduh@cs.jhu.edu

Xuan Zhang
Johns Hopkins University
Baltimore, USA
xuanzhang@jhu.edu

1 Brief Description

Automated Machine Learning (AutoML) is an emerging field that has potential to impact how we build models in NLP. As an umbrella term that includes topics like **hyperparameter optimization** and **neural architecture search**, AutoML has recently become mainstream at major conferences such as NeurIPS, ICML, and ICLR. The inaugural AutoML Conference[1] was started in 2022, and with this community effort, we expect that deep learning software frameworks will begin to include AutoML functionality in the near future.

What does this mean to NLP? Currently, models are often built in an ad hoc process: we might borrow default hyperparameters from previous work and try a few variant architectures, but it is never guaranteed that final trained model is optimal. Automation can introduce rigor in this model-building process. For example, hyperparameter optimization can help NLP *researchers* find reasonably accurate models under limited computation budget, leading to fairer comparison of proposed and baseline methods. Similarly, neural architecture search can help NLP *developers* discover models with the desired speed-accuracy tradeoffs for deployment.

This tutorial will summarize the main AutoML techniques and illustrate how to apply them to improve the NLP model-building process. The goal is to provide the audience with the necessary background to follow and use AutoML research in their own work.

Type of tutorial: Cutting-Edge[2]

2 Target Audience

The tutorial is aimed at NLP researchers and developers who have experience in building deep learning models and are interested in exploring the potential of AutoML in improving their system-building process. Recommended prerequisites are:

- NLP: Familiarity with common neural networks used in the field, especially the Transformer architecture.
- Machine Learning: Understanding of classical supervised learning. Knowledge of Bayesian and Evolutionary methods will be a plus, but not required.
- Programming: Basic experience with training models in deep learning frameworks like PyTorch or Tensorflow.

3 Tutorial Content

Outline: This is a 3-hour tutorial. It is divided into two parts:

1. Overview of major AutoML techniques
   (a) Hyperparameter optimization
   (b) Neural architecture search
2. Application of AutoML to NLP
   (a) Evaluation
   (b) Multiple objectives for deployment
   (c) Cost and carbon footprint
   (d) Software design best practices
   (e) Literature survey

In Part 1, we will focus on two major sub-areas within AutoML: Hyperparameter optimization is the problem of finding optimal hyperparameters, such as learning rate of gradient descent and embedding size of Transformers, based on past training experience. Neural architecture search is the problem of designing the optimal combination of neural network components in a fined-grained fashion. We will summarize these rapidly developing fields and

[1] https://2022.automl.cc
[2] Tutorial Website: https://www.cs.jhu.edu/~kevinduh/a/automl-tutorial-2023/

Proceedings of the 17th Conference of the European Chapter of the Association for Computational Linguistics
Tutorial Abstracts, pages 25–26
May 2-4, 2023

explain several representative algorithms, including Bayesian Optimization, Evolutionary Strategies, Population-Based Training, Asynchronous Hyperband, and DARTS.

Part 2 will discuss the practical issues of applying AutoML research to NLP. Questions we will seek to answer include: (a) How do we evaluate AutoML methods on NLP tasks? (b) How can we extend AutoML methods to deployment situations that require multiple objectives, such as inference speed and test accuracy? (c) What is the cost (and carbon footprint) of these methods, and when will it be worthwhile? (d) How should we design our model-building software given a specific computing environment, and what existing tools are available?

Reading List: The tutorial will be self-contained, so there is no required reading list. For a preview of the techniques we will cover, the audience is welcomed to refer to survey papers such as (Feurer and Hutter, 2019; Elsken et al., 2019).

We gave a similar tutorial titled "AutoML for Machine Translation" at AMTA 2022, a machine translation conference. The tutorial slides are available[3]. For the EACL tutorial, we will add discussion on recent uses of AutoML in various NLP applications, ranging from text classification to large language models.

4 Presenters

Kevin Duh is a senior research scientist at the Johns Hopkins University Human Language Technology Center of Excellence (HLTCOE) and an assistant research professor in the Department of Computer Science. His research interests lie at the intersection of NLP and Machine Learning. He has given several conference tutorials on the topics of machine learning and machine translation at, e.g., AMTA 2022, SLTU 2018, IJCNN 2017, DL4MT Winter School 2015.

Xuan Zhang is a Ph.D. student in the Department of Computer Science at Johns Hopkins University (JHU). She performs research in Machine Translation, with specific interests in Sign Language Translation, Hyperparameter Optimization, Curriculum Learning, and Domain Adaptation. She co-presented the AMTA 2022 tutorial on AutoML.

[3] `https://www.cs.jhu.edu/~kevinduh/notes/2209-AMTA-AutoMLtutorial.pdf`

5 Ethics Statement

There are at least three concerns relevant for responsible use of AutoML technology.

- Energy: Improper use of AutoML may lead to wasted computation in the extreme, e.g. training of thousands of neural models that are eventually discarded. That is why we feel it is important in the tutorial to include a section on cost and carbon footprint.
- Jobs: Some worry that AutoML may reduce the need for data scientists. It is true that some of the black magic involved in hyperparameter and architecture tuning is taken away by AutoML, but we believe that AutoML tools will relieve data scientists to focus on more interesting problems regarding the underlying task, similar to how auto-differentiation tools revolutionized deep learning.
- Bias: If there are underlying biases in the training data, AutoML may output a "optimized" model that exacerbates the bias more so than a manual model-building process. It is thus even more important to check for fairness and bias in an AutoML setup.

References

Thomas Elsken, Jan Hendrik Metzen, and Frank Hutter. 2019. Neural architecture search: A survey. *Journal of Machine Learning Research*, 20(55):1–21.

Matthias Feurer and Frank Hutter. 2019. *Hyperparameter Optimization*, chapter 1. Springer.

Tutorial on Privacy-Preserving Natural Language Processing

Ivan Habernal[1] **Fatemehsadat Mireshghallah**[2] **Patricia Thaine**[3]
Sepideh Ghanavati[4] **Oluwaseyi Feyisetan**[5]

[1]Trustworthy Human Language Technologies, Technical University of Darmstadt
[2]Computer Science and Engineering Department, University of California San Diego
[3]Private AI, Canada
[4]School of Computing and Information Science, University of Maine
[5]Meta, USA

Abstract

This cutting-edge tutorial will help the NLP community to get familiar with current research in privacy-preserving methods. We will cover topics as diverse as membership inference, differential privacy, homomorphic encryption, or federated learning, all with typical applications to NLP. The goal is not only to draw the interest of the broader community, but also to present some typical use-cases and potential pitfalls in applying privacy-preserving methods to human language technologies.

1 Introduction

Human language technologies play an essential role in the modern society. From automatic machine translation to drug discovery, NLP has had an undeniable impact on everyone's life. However, many of the recent achievements of state-of-the-art models come at a price that everyone must pay. In the race for yet better performing systems, the research has completely ignored the fact that within the extreme amounts of data needed for the 'hungry' models, there are private information of actual living persons (Carlini et al., 2020). Our sensitive information – be it explicitly mentioned in the texts we or someone else writes about us, or implicitly in our writing style – is at stake with current NLP models. Privacy matters a lot to society, but has been largely neglected by NLP researchers.

This tutorial aims to close this gap by offering the community insights into state-of-the-art approaches to privacy-preserving NLP. We will cover diverse topics, such as membership inference, differential privacy, homomorphic encryption, or federated learning, all with typical use-cases and applications. The tutorial will try to balance theoretical foundations with practical considerations.

2 Tutorial outline

We propose a **half-day** tutorial (3 hours) divided into four following thematic blocks.

2.1 Block 1: Attacks (30 minutes)

This block will provide an overview why differential privacy is needed by introducing and discussing reconstruction attacks and examples of difference attacks (Dinur and Nissim, 2003). We will discuss how an algorithm can be blatantly non-private via an example from census data and explain inefficient and efficient attacks. We then discuss reconstruction attacks in practice for several cases (Cohen and Nissim, 2020). We conclude this block by briefly explaining some examples of tracing attacks (Homer et al., 2008) and (Dwork et al., 2015).

2.2 Block 2a: Defence with formal guarantees (60 min)

This block will introduce differential privacy, a mathematical framework for privacy protection (Dwork and Roth, 2013). We will explain the typical setup (why this privacy approach has 'differential' in its title) and the formal definitions. Then we will address some basic DP mechanisms and show their NLP applications. This part will involve a few mathematical proofs, but our aim is to make it low-barrier and accessible to a very broad audience.

In the second part, we will introduce some cryptographic tools, namely homomorphic encryption and secure multiparty computation. The main focus will be on introducing the basics of lattice-based cryptography and homomorphic encryption and the most popular schemes (BGV, CKKS). We will go over the available libraries (PALISADE, HElib, SEAL) and dive into an NLP-specific example.

Proceedings of the 17th Conference of the European Chapter of the Association for Computational Linguistics
Tutorial Abstracts, pages 27–30

2.3 Block 2b: Defences without formal guarantees (20 min)

Apart from privacy-preserving schemes that directly optimize for a given definition of privacy, there are given execution models and environments that help enhance privacy and are not by themselves privacy-preserving in a formal sense. This block will introduce privacy-enhancing methods such as federated learning (McMahan et al., 2017), split learning (Vepakomma et al., 2018) and regularizer-based methods (Coavoux et al., 2018; Mireshghallah et al.; Li et al., 2018).

Federated learning and split learning are both based on distributed learning and are great methods for application in enterprise and clinical setups. Regularizer based and private representation learning methods add extra terms to the loss function to limit the memorization and encoding of sensitive data within the model.

2.4 Block 3: Privacy in industry (40 min)

Companies have practical constraints when deploying privacy preserving technologies. Some of these include deployment and computation at scale, or guarantees that solutions meet compliance or regulatory requirements. There is also the trade-off between privacy, utility, bias, fairness, (Farrand et al., 2020) as well as explainability and verifiability of the implemented solutions.

In this section, we will dive deep into different technologies and discuss their trade-offs from an industry perspective. We will also highlight how the community can help accelerate progress along different dimensions.

2.5 Block 4: Open problems in privacy in NLP (30 min)

We will talks some further NLP specifics, such as (1) perturbing long-form text with differential privacy without losing the content, and (2) introducing better auditing methods for measuring memorization in discriminative and generative large language models (BERT or GPT based models).

3 Reading list

- Joseph P. Near and Chiké Abuah. 2021. *Programming Differential Privacy*. Online, https://uvm-plaid.github.io/programming-dp/
- (Optional) Cynthia Dwork and Aaron Roth. 2013. The Algorithmic Foundations of Differential Privacy. *Foundations and Trends® in Theoretical Computer Science*, 9(3-4):211–407

4 Tutorial specifics

The proposed tutorial is considered a **cutting-edge** tutorial that presents recent advances in an emerging area of privacy-preserving techniques for NLP. The topic presented has not been covered in previous ACL*-family tutorials in the last 4 years. We estimate that at least 60% of the papers covered in this tutorial are from researchers other than the instructors. It is also **different** from other tutorials, e.g., on differentially-private machine learning, as we target NLP with all its peculiarities related to human language.

The **preferred venue** for this tutorial would be 1) ACL, 2) EACL, 3) EMNLP. We prefer ACL due to travel arrangements of presenters located in the U.S.

Based on the raising interest in this topic, we expect around 30 participants. The tutorial will be **self-contained**, however attendees should have solid **background** in basic deep learning technologies in NLP (representations, architectures, optimization)[1] and to brush up knowledge of probability and statistics (Laplace or Gaussian distributions and probability bounds).[2]

We are committed to **open-source** all teaching materials under permissible license.

5 Tutorial presenters

Diversity considerations:

- 4 academia and 2 industry affiliations
- 3 female instructors
- Participation of senior (up to Assistant Professor) and junior (PhD candidate) instructors

Details of the organizing committee are included below in alphabetical order.

Oluwaseyi Feyisetan (Meta, USA)

Seyi is a Staff Research Scientist at Facebook. Prior to Facebook, he was a Senior Applied Scientist at Amazon where he worked on Differential Privacy in the context of NLP. He holds 4 pending patents

[1]For example (Goldberg, 2017)

[2]For example Chapter 1–4 and 8–9 from (Mitzenmacher and Upfal, 2017)

with Amazon on preserving privacy in NLP systems. He completed his PhD at the University of Southampton in the UK and has published in top tier conferences and journals on crowdsourcing, homomorphic encryption, and privacy. He has served as a reviewer at top NLP conferences including ACL and EMNLP. Prior to Amazon, he spent 7 years in the UK where he worked at different startups and institutions focusing on regulatory compliance, machine learning and NLP within the finance sector. He also sits on the research advisory board of the IAPP.

Sepideh Ghanavati (University of Maine, USA)

Assistant professor in Computer Science at the University of Maine. She is the director of Privacy Engineering - Regulatory Compliance Lab (PERC_Lab). Her research interests are in the areas of information privacy and security, software engineering, machine learning and the Internet of Things (IoT). Previously, she worked as an assistant professor at Texas Tech University, visiting assistant professor at Radboud University, the Netherlands and as a visiting faculty at Carnegie Mellon University. She is the recipient of Google Faculty Research award in 2018. She has more than 10 years of academic and industry experience in the area of privacy and regulatory compliance and has published more than 30 peer-reviewed publications. She was a co-organizer of the 'Privacy and Language Technologies' at the 2019 AAAI Spring Symposium and has been part of the organizing committee of several workshops and conferences in the past.

Ivan Habernal (Technische Universität Darmstadt, Germany)

Ivan Habernal is currently leading a junior independent research group at the Technical University of Darmstadt, Germany, funded ad-personam by the state of Hessen. His group entitled "Trustworthy Human Language Technologies" focuses on privacy-preserving NLP and legal argument mining, among others. He has a track of top NLP publications (h-index 19), chairing workshops and tutorials, area chairing, organizing SemEval competition, giving invited talks, and also some recent industrial experience in areas where privacy matters a lot but the tools are not ready yet (healthcare and online personalization).

Fatemeh Mireshghallah (University of California, USA)

Fatemehsadat Mireshghallah is a Ph.D. student at the CSE department of UC San Diego. Her research interests are Trustworthy Machine Learning and Natural Language Processing. She received her B.S. from Sharif university of technology in Iran. She is a recipient of the National Center for Women & IT (NCWIT) Collegiate award in 2020 for her work on privacy-preserving inference, and a finalist of the Qualcomm Innovation Fellowship in 2021. She has interned twice at Microsoft Research's Language and Intelligent Assistance group, where she worked on private training of large language models. She is also serving as a NAACL 2022 D&I co-chair and WiNLP committee member.

Patricia Thaine (University of Toronto, Canada)

Patricia Thaine is the Co-Founder and CEO of Private AI, a Computer Science PhD Candidate at the University of Toronto and a Postgraduate Affiliate at the Vector Institute doing research on privacy-preserving natural language processing, with a focus on applied cryptography. She also does research on computational methods for lost language decipherment. Patricia is a recipient of the NSERC Postgraduate Scholarship, the RBC Graduate Fellowship, the Beatrice 'Trixie' Worsley Graduate Scholarship in Computer Science, and the Ontario Graduate Scholarship. She has eight years of research and software development experience, including at the McGill Language Development Lab, the University of Toronto's Computational Linguistics Lab, the University of Toronto's Department of Linguistics, and the Public Health Agency of Canada. She is the Co-Founder and CEO of Private AI, the former President of the Computer Science Graduate Student Union at the University of Toronto, and a member of the Board of Directors of Equity Showcase, one of Canada's oldest not-for-profit charitable organizations.

References

Nicholas Carlini, Florian Tramer, Eric Wallace, Matthew Jagielski, Ariel Herbert-Voss, Katherine Lee, Adam Roberts, Tom Brown, Dawn Song, Ulfar Erlingsson, Alina Oprea, and Colin Raffel. 2020. Extracting Training Data from Large Language Models. *arXiv preprint*.

Maximin Coavoux, Shashi Narayan, and Shay B. Cohen. 2018. Privacy-preserving neural representations of text. In *Proceedings of the 2018 Conference on Empirical Methods in Natural Language Processing*, pages 1–10, Brussels, Belgium. Association for Computational Linguistics.

Aloni Cohen and Kobbi Nissim. 2020. Linear program reconstruction in practice. *J. Priv. Confidentiality*, 10.

Irit Dinur and Kobbi Nissim. 2003. Revealing information while preserving privacy. In *Proceedings of the Twenty-Second ACM SIGMOD-SIGACT-SIGART Symposium on Principles of Database Systems*, PODS '03, page 202–210, New York, NY, USA. Association for Computing Machinery.

Cynthia Dwork and Aaron Roth. 2013. The Algorithmic Foundations of Differential Privacy. *Foundations and Trends® in Theoretical Computer Science*, 9(3-4):211–407.

Cynthia Dwork, Adam D. Smith, Thomas Steinke, Jonathan R. Ullman, and Salil P. Vadhan. 2015. Robust traceability from trace amounts. In *IEEE 56th Annual Symposium on Foundations of Computer Science, FOCS 2015, Berkeley, CA, USA, 17-20 October, 2015*, pages 650–669. IEEE Computer Society.

Tom Farrand, Fatemehsadat Mireshghallah, Sahib Singh, and Andrew Trask. 2020. Neither private nor fair: Impact of data imbalance on utility and fairness in differential privacy. In *Proceedings of the 2020 Workshop on Privacy-Preserving Machine Learning in Practice*, pages 15–19.

Yoav Goldberg. 2017. *Neural Network Methods for Natural Language Processing*. Morgan & Claypool Publishers.

N. Homer, S. Szelinger, M. Redman, D. Duggan, W. Tembe, J. Muehling, J. V. Pearson, D. A. Stephan, S. F. Nelson, and D. W. Craig. 2008. Resolving individuals contributing trace amounts of dna to highly complex mixtures using high-density snp genotyping microarrays. *PLoS genetics*, 4.

Yitong Li, Timothy Baldwin, and Trevor Cohn. 2018. Towards robust and privacy-preserving text representations. In *ACL*.

H. Brendan McMahan, Daniel Ramage, Kunal Talwar, and Li Zhang. 2017. Learning differentially private language models without losing accuracy. *ArXiv*, abs/1710.06963.

Fatemehsadat Mireshghallah, Huseyin A Inan, Marcello Hasegawa, Victor Rühle, Taylor Berg-Kirkpatrick, and Robert Sim. Privacy regularization: Joint privacy-utility optimization in language models.

Michael Mitzenmacher and Eli Upfal. 2017. *Probability and Computing: Randomization and Probabilistic Techniques in Algorithms and Data Analysis*, 2nd edition. Cambridge University Press.

Joseph P. Near and Chiké Abuah. 2021. *Programming Differential Privacy*. Online, https://uvm-plaid.github.io/programming-dp/.

Praneeth Vepakomma, Otkrist Gupta, Tristan Swedish, and Ramesh Raskar. 2018. Split learning for health: Distributed deep learning without sharing raw patient data. *ArXiv*, abs/1812.00564.

Author Index